CRISIS
INTERVENTION
VERBATIM

CRISIS INTERVENTION VERBATIM

Nira Kfir
Maagalim Institute of Psychotherapy
and Counseling in Adlerian Psychology
Tel Aviv, Israel

Edited by
Janet R. Terner

● HEMISPHERE PUBLISHING CORPORATION
A member of the Taylor & Francis Group
New York   Washington   Philadelphia   London

CRISIS INTERVENTION VERBATIM

1 2 3 4 5 6 7 8 9 0   B R B R   8 9 8 7 6 5 4 3 2 1 0 9

This book was set in Century by WorldComp.
Cover design by Tammy Marshall.
Braun-Brumfield was printer and binder.

Library of Congress Cataloging-in-Publication Data

Kfir, Nira
    Crisis intervention verbatim / Nira Kfir; with the editorial
assistance of Janet Terner.
      p.   cm.
    Bibliography: p.
    Includes index.

    1. Crisis intervention (Psychiatry) 2. Crisis intervention
(Psychiatry)—Case studies. I. Terner, Janet R. II. Title.
RC480.6.K47 1988   88-19806
362.2'8—dc19   CIP
ISBN 0-89116-837-0

*This book is lovingly dedicated
to my parents,
Devora and David Lipmanovich*

Contents

Foreword

Sometimes the timing of events in life is fortuitous. For example, I received a copy of Nira Kfir's book, *Crisis Intervention Verbatim,* on a certain day. Before I had a chance to read it, a former client called me for an emergency session and appeared with her adult daughter. I had seen this client for another emergency about 3 months before due to her catastrophic reaction to the impending death of her father. And now I found out that her mother had no more than 3 months to live, having cancer (as had her father)—and my client again was in crisis.

As before, she was in tears; she complained that she was alone, that her stoic family would not allow her to cry, and that she could not face the future without her mother—her best friend. All attempts by her daughter and other relatives failed to console this distraught woman.

Therapists faced by such problems, frequently attempt—

as I did, out of ignorance of what to do—to have the patient talk it out. Usually we wind up giving advice and consolation which generally are not listened to and are rejected out of hand. When the two left, all of us probably drained by the session's high degree of emotionality, I had a feeling that somehow I had not really been of much help.

On the next day, I opened the package of Dr. Kfir's manuscript, sent to me by Janet Terner for my reading. About halfway through my reading, it struck me that this was the very book for this client: I called her, asked her to come to my office at her convenience. She came that very day, read it with great avidity, and on finishing it thanked me with the strongest expressions of appreciation. She stated that reading this book gave her understanding and surcease.

Consequently, I learned that this book, intended primarily for professional people such as physicians, attorneys, ministers, psychologists, social workers, psychiatrists, and counselors of all types, is certainly helpful even for people in crisis. I recommend it as an auxiliary tool.

But to come to a broader comment about this book and its author:

In Japan they have a charming custom of declaring certain individuals national treasures. In my judgment Dr. Nira Kfir is such. It is infrequent that in one person are found knowledge, good sense, balance, and the ability to see beyond boundaries and make things happen. Such indeed is Nira Kfir, a friend of many years, the developer of the basic personality concept of priorities, a counselor and psychotherapist par excellence, a mover and a shaker.

Crises often result in suicide or other devastating consequences. A person in a crisis is in this state exactly because he or she does not know how to cope, and most people who are in the life space of that person usually do not know what to do. All attempts to comfort the individual or alleviate the situation do not work.

It is ironic that a professional person who is put into interaction with a person in crisis and who does not know what to do finds himself or herself also in a crisis situation! It is the blind leading the blind.

Crisis Intervention Verbatim, with its two part approach of theory and practice (through case histories), is truly a magnificent document which can be of considerable help to professional people dealing with crisis situations through giving them an understanding of the basic mechanisms of crises and an appreciation of effective ways of handling such problems. Consequently, it should be read for its wisdom by all people who deal with crises—whether on a short-term basis, such as policemen and soldiers do, or on a long-term basis, such as psychotherapists do.

I would be remiss not to comment on the partnership that Dr. Kfir has with Janet Terner in the writing of this book. Nira Kfir, fluent in several languages, is a most effective speaker in English, which is not her native language. However, to convert spoken English into written English is a special skill and it is this contribution that Mrs. Terner made to this book. After all, what good is understanding if it cannot be communicated effectively? This book is a model of clear writing as well as good sense.

I end with the thought that, regardless of one's philosophical or theoretical position, this book transcends narrow partisanship and addresses the needs of all people in crisis and of those who try to meet the needs of others in crisis. It belongs in the library or on the desk of all who deal with crises and should be available also to those individuals in a crisis situation as an auxiliary aid.

Raymond J. Corsini, Ph.D.
Honolulu

Preface

This book on crisis intervention grew directly from a 2-week course taught in London, England, in 1986 under the sponsorship of the British Association of Social Psychiatry and the Association of Adlerian Workshops. It reflects, however, a theory of understanding crisis and a process of intervention that evolved over many years, beginning with my work with bereaved families in Israel following the 1973 Yom Kippur War. Its theoretical underpinnings are based on the wealth of wisdom I acquired from my teachers, chief among them the late Rudolf Dreikurs, who restored the practical, common-sense psychological approach of Alfred Adler. Their influence and training blended together to guide my work as a psychotherapist and inspired my thinking on the nature of the therapeutic process, its goals, and new methods for reaching out to people gripped by distress, impasse, depression, crisis.

For more than 2 decades I have directed a psychothera-

peutic clinic and trained its staff. Our efforts as a cohesive
working team led to efficient and reliable new techniques for
diagnosis and treatment. These techniques gave rise to my
concept of the priorities, which became the basis of a new model
of personality theory, the Impasse/Priority Therapy (IPT). They
also paved the way for the crisis intervention model presented
here.

In 1985, when the Maagalim Institute of Tel Aviv was
founded, I was able to implement a long-nurtured dream,
namely, to create a free walk-in crisis intervention center. In
the years since its founding, the center has offered help to a
steady stream of distressed persons of all ages. From a his-
torical perspective, this center is a modern version of Alfred
Adler's pioneering suicide intervention clinics in Vienna in
the early decades of this century.

There is little doubt that the stresses and uncertainties of
life in today's highly complex and technical world are crisis
provoking. The need to teach professionals and laypersons
about the nature of crisis, how crisis impacts the individual,
and how best to help and guide its victims back to a sense of
equilibrium is abundantly recognized and the object of this
work. This book is composed of two sections. The first part
contains a theoretical exploration of the nature of crisis, and
the second part includes verbatim transcripts of actual clients
in crisis who volunteered to participate in the London workshop for a one-time intervention session. I believe that as one
reads their stories and reflects on them it becomes apparent
how effective even a single intervention opportunity can be
in helping the person move through the stages of crisis.

Workshops such as this one and the people who come to
them, whether as volunteer counselees or as course participants (physicians, social workers, nurses, therapists, and hos-
pice or crisis hotline workers), provide a unique forum where
all can learn firsthand the common threads of the crisis experience. The crisis might be brought on by the death or loss
of a beloved person, the impasse of a lifestyle that will not
work, the knowledge of terminal illness, or a host of other
possibilities. The volunteer counselees who allowed us to record the sessions and use their stories have made a genuine

contribution toward helping us better understand crisis and assist those caught in its maelstrom to survive it and, I hope, to gain a new freedom and empowerment from the process.

Nira Kfir
Tel Aviv, Israel

Acknowledgments

I want to acknowledge the people who made this book possible. There were many, including some unknown to me personally—people in bereavement, group members, people who came to the center, authors of books that I read at the right moment. I want to thank them all and express my appreciation for their contribution.

I also want to express my gratitude to my London friends and colleagues who provided the setting that enabled this book to reach fruition. Special acknowledgment goes to Dr. Lilianne Beattie, who encouraged and organized the crisis workshop, and to Neil Ajmal of Adlerian Workshops and Publications, who produced the original transcripts of the lectures and case presentations. Dr. Maurice Slevin, Heddi and Robert Wax, Beverly Seligson, and others were particularly helpful by bringing clients and patients to be counseled. Without the trust and efforts of these people the workshops and this book could not have happened.

I also want to acknowledge my colleagues and friends who joined me in starting Maagalim, our therapy institute and crisis center in Tel Aviv. Together we experienced that rare moment of transformation from crisis to change. I am especially grateful to Tilly Milner, the first reader and critic of this text, whose intuitive reactions and suggestions I learned to accept and rely on.

Deep gratitude goes to Ray Corsini, a friend and colleague of many years, who encouraged my writing and generously gave his time to critique my work. He has been a genuine "think tank partner," never failing to exchange ideas freely at every opportunity—whether at meetings in far-flung places around the world, through the mail, or by telephone between Tel Aviv and Honolulu.

To Janet Terner, with whom I share a flow between minds that makes writer and editor slip into reverse roles, my appreciation is expressed for her tireless efforts to refine the manuscript and for the wonderful energy she stimulates.

And last, I want to thank my family—my husband and many years friend, Motti, and my children, Shirly (her husband, Danny) and Effrat. They have been wonderful listeners and put up with so many crisis stories over the years. My deep love and gratitude go to them for all their support and love.

Introduction

In 1942, when I was 4 years old, our home was perched on a hill overlooking Haifa Bay in what was then called Palestine. The bay was under heavy bombardment by German-Italian aircraft determined to destroy the oil refineries.

I remember vividly the night they finally succeeded in hitting the refinery. We came out of the shelters—although the bombing was still underway—and stood in our small yard to watch the distant refinery tanks all ablaze. The sky that night was red, the smell of oil and the black smoke wafted up as a noxious cloud, and the feeling of impending disaster filled our hearts. One feeling from that moment is still alive. It is a feeling beyond fear, of utter despair.

As morning dawned, my parents made a quick decision they didn't dare consider before—that we must leave Haifa and that we must separate. My father would stay behind to find whatever work was available to support us, and my mother, my 15-year-old sister, and I would move to Jerusalem. We left that very morning carrying all our belongings in two suitcases (little more than my parents brought with them from Poland just 7 years earlier).

Jerusalem, the city "they" would not dare bomb, lay clean and awash in sunshine. Penniless and homeless, we were supposed to find a certain middle-aged couple, friends of friends back in Poland. They lived in a one-room flat without either a kitchen or a toilet, in a building at 5 Alafandri Street. My mother carried a note from friends introducing us to these people. Tired and hungry, we arrived at their door late that afternoon. We knocked. Someone said, "It's open," and we entered.

Unlike Jerusalem's aura of light, which struck me so indelibly in the street, the room was dark. Two people—who seemed very old to me—a man with a long beard and a woman with a kerchief that totally covered her hair, looked up at us from two big cushions on the floor. I don't remember how it was told to us, but they had lost their only son that same week and were holding *Shiva,* the traditional 7 days of mourning. That meant sitting on the floor, not closing the door of the house to visitors, and not greeting us with the usual *shalom.*

In this room, which contained one double bed, a sofa, a table and chairs, a wardrobe, and one window, we spent the next 6 months as guests of these bereaved strangers. This one room held their tragedy and ours, their aloneness in life and our loneliness in a new city, their final separation and our temporary one from home and father. Their need for family warmth and ours met. A new life was born for our family. Jerusalem nourished us with everything we later became.

This was my first experience of crisis and change.

This book presents a theoretical model of crisis intervention and actual cases from a workshop conducted in London in March 1986. The model was first shaped under the pressure of a profound national and human crisis that touched thousands of lives—the Yom Kippur War of October 1973.

In the summer of 1973 I was writing a summary report of

a 3-year project for the Rehabilitation Department of the Israel Ministry of Defense. We had been supervising the senior staff responsible for treating war widows, wounded soldiers, and bereaved parents. We summed up our work with a recommended model of intervention and counseling for the bereaved. I finished the report and submitted my recommendations to the ministry on the eve of Yom Kippur that year with the hope that we would never need to implement any of them.

The Yom Kippur War broke out the next day. Close to midnight, while I was watching the fast-breaking news on TV, the head of the ministry's rehabilitation department phoned to ask if I would stand behind my 1-day-old report. I replied affirmatively, and he then requested that I work with them to put my plan into action. My recommendations were based on a theoretical model drawn from my work with the rehabilitation staff and my direct experiences as a therapist. They had never been tested under the conditions of sudden, widespread tragedy and loss that befell Israel in 1973. I was afraid that night, dreading the possibility most psychologists who construct theories dream about—namely, the opportunity to prove my theory in practice. Only I didn't want to prove it.

At 7:00 the next morning, I appeared at the ministry's headquarters in an old Jaffa building. Telephones rang continuously, people were running frantically from office to office, all the radios were turned on, blaring the latest reports from the front. I listened as the first casualty reports began filtering in, knowing that more and more were yet to come, gripped by that awful feeling of awaiting a job I didn't want to touch.

The names poured in. In such a small country, every name sounds familiar, every family counts, and every family feels the impact. It became very clear that we would be faced with a large number of families suffering sudden loss at the same time. No model for treating widespread bereavement existed, and there were very little literature on the subject and few experts to consult. We sought advice from psychologists who held esteemed chairs in well-known universities and from foreign government agencies like the Pentagon in Washington. We were eager to learn how other countries dealt with the problem of bereavement. To our disappointment we found out that very little was done and no structured model of intervention existed at the time.

So we had to structure our own program of intervention. Shortly, one of the army's senior social workers was at my side to assist in putting the plan into practice. She worked closely with me and my staff for a whole year. We recruited 500 volunteers, trained and supervised them, and through them reached out to every bereaved family. We started special support groups for the bereaved and met the face of grief and bereavement many times every day.

The 500 volunteers included both trained professionals and others who had only their *bonne voluntee* to offer. There was no time for adequate psychological training because of the pressing need to make contact with the bereaved families before their grief and pain compelled them to close the door to life forever. The volunteers were formed into pairs and they fanned out over the whole country to make house calls. Each pair treated six families and visited them once a week for an entire year.

As part of the model, groups of bereaved parents were formed and led by the volunteers. The prevailing professional opinion was that if bereaved people are brought together in a group they will behave autistically because they are totally wrapped up in their own sorrow and unable to give support to others. Our work proved that notion to be wrong.

We assumed the groups would work because they offered an excellent setting for people in crisis to receive information, support, and options—ingredients essential to their resumption of normal life. They received (1) *information* about the grieving process and its impact on life, family relations, siblings, sex, and hope; (2) *support* through the involvement of the community and the presence of other bereaved persons; and (3) *options*—ways to pursue recovery and change, to gain the advantage of seeing things from a new perspective that could not be seen before.

Trained group leaders hesitated for lack of experience to lead these groups. We were forced to pursue a unique opportunity—to start these groups with volunteers and community functioneers (nurses, teachers, rabbis, and laypersons) as group leaders. The volunteer leaders were supervised in a large group once a week. By the end of the year, they succeeded in developing 28 groups for bereaved parents in Tel Aviv alone. Some of these groups have evolved in a variety of ways and continue to meet to this day. At the same time, the Ministry of Defense created a special unit to treat bereaved parents based on this model and it is still used today to train professionals and laypersons.

Over the years, this model was developed by our clinic staff to serve all manner of crisis situations and interventions and also influenced our therapeutic approach. Psychotherapy, being a form of intervention, follows this same model, and my prediction is that in the next decade or so all therapy will become intervention oriented.

The people whose lives and crises are told here present a variety of life's pitfalls, traps, and blows, whether caused by man or nature. Our purpose was to demonstrate a one-time intervention strategy in crisis caused by anxiety, bereavement, terminal disease, drugs, and melancholia. Some of the people who came made us stand in awe of the human spirit. They were as great in encouraging us as we tried to be to them.

Workshops such as this one and the people who came, either as participants or as counselees, offer hope and evidence that our society is moving forward to a time when we'll become again "our brother's keeper."

Nira Kfir
Tel Aviv, Israel

I

THEORY AND MODEL OF CRISIS INTERVENTION

1

Nature of Crisis

Individuals of all ages, cultures, and backgrounds can suffer a severe crisis brought on by a variety of situations. What constitutes a crisis and how to distinguish whether a person is in crisis or undergoing a stressful period in life are issues that confront nearly all of us—as professionals, friends, family members. When to intervene and, more importantly, how to intervene when someone is suffering through a crisis are challenging and timely issues addressed in this work.

The *American Heritage Dictionary* (1973) defines *crisis* as "the turning point for better or for worse in an acute disease; a paroxysmal attack of pain, distress or disordered function; [and] an emotionally significant event or radical change of status in a person's life." A simple working definition of crisis is *whatever radically disturbs and upsets the normal order of a person's life*. The well-being of an individual or a community depends on dealing with a crisis before it degenerates into a

3

disaster and preventing crises, as far as possible, before they happen.

A crisis, then, is a state a person reaches as a result of trauma. That trauma can be externally inflicted or due to an inner development. In all cases, the onset of a crisis is not a direct reaction to whatever has happened to the person, but rather his or her interpretation of the situation or event. Behavior follows interpretation and, in turn, justifies it.

Illness, the death of a dear one, rape, assault, loss of property, and uprooting of any kind are not, in themselves, triggers of crisis. They may, in fact, become triggers of strength. People under various stresses—war, disease, failure, poverty, dramatic change in conditions—may instead be stimulated to resourcefulness, to a recruitment of inner strength, to endurance of unbelievable physical feats, and also to a breakthrough to a new understanding. A breakthrough under severe stress is a victory that means growth and enrichment. But a stressful or traumatic event, interpreted differently, may instead trigger crisis.

CRISIS VERSUS A STRESSFUL PERIOD

Differentiating between a *crisis* and a *stressful period in life* is not merely a matter of definition. A situation that can result in crisis for one individual, another individual can take in stride. Innumerable situations have the potential to provoke a crisis. Most of us experience what it is like to be in crisis at least once in our lives.

A stressful period poses a challenge, an opportunity to grow, to develop more of our potential. We accomplish more, function on less sleep, work efficiently under pressure, and survive without support. To our amazement, we often discover we accomplished things we never believed we could do. A stressful period evokes tension and anxiety and usually involves a conflict that must be resolved, a problem that requires new behaviors in order to be solved, and always the elements of uncertainty and the unknown. Because we are breaking ground to solve a new problem, we seek and absorb a lot of information. We recruit advice and assistance from family, friends, or any available source.

A stressful period can, of course, develop into a crisis, so it is important to distinguish those characteristics common to a person in a state of crisis. They are:

1. emotional shock
2. a demand to change one's regular behavior
3. a demand for immediate action or intervention
4. the confrontation of a totally new phenomenon (the situation itself may not be so terrible but the fact that it is confronted for the *first time* makes it a crisis)
5. the loss of the ability to think rationally or to integrate new information
6. a break in the person's system of values
7. a feeling of reaching "dead end" with no sense of how to proceed
8. unpredictability—both for the person who experiences the crisis and those who observe the situation

Crisis situations are totally new, unpredictable, psychologically paralyzing, and they pose a shock to the emotional system. They catch the victim unprepared and lacking a ready response. The absence of a repertoire of responses that have worked in the past is most disturbing because we spend much of our daily lives operating on "automatic pilot," relying on tried and tested behaviors.

PREDISPOSITIONS FOR CRISIS

Even extremely painful situations such as the death or fatal illness of a beloved do not universally result in crisis. For some individuals this would certainly be the predictable result. But for many others, these situations prove to be extremely stressful without developing into a crisis. The question that naturally arises is what character elements or personality traits make some persons more susceptible to crisis than others. Working with individuals in crisis over several decades, I have found three major issues that affect a person's predisposition to crisis. They are (1) the person's existential under-standing of psychic survival, which I call the *number one priority*, (2) his or her personal history of a previous unresolved disaster, and (3) the person's distorted view of "balance in life" including a negative attitude toward change.

Number One Priority*

The individuality of each person emerges from the specific combination and integration of character elements. This in-

---

*I developed the Impasse and Personality Priorities therapeutic system and my clinical staff and I have used it for more than a decade. It has proven to be an effective tool for elucidating the lifestyle, for diagnostic purposes, and for designing therapy or counseling programs that facilitate growth and movement.

According to this system, impasses are roadblocks that evolve in early child-hood and impede or limit the child's social development and movement in life. Impasses develop out of a coalescence of unpleasant or painful interpersonal experiences in early life that signify nonsignificance and nonbelonging to the child. The basic impasse situations are:

1. *Rejection:* The fear of not being wanted or appreciated, of being avoided
2. *Insignificance:* The fear of being unimportant, worthless, meaningless
3. *Ridicule:* The fear of humiliation, of appearing stupid, inept, or foolish
4. *Stress:* The fear of conflict, unrelenting pressure, danger

These impasse situations developmentally lead to creation of the priorities, behavioral strategies that will assure a sense of belonging and significance to the individual. The priorities, which are incorporated into the person's uniquely fash-ioned personality or lifestyle, are:

1. *Pleasing:* To avoid rejection, pleasers seek constant acceptance and approval and can be very self-sacrificing in their efforts to secure them.
2. *Moral superiority:* To avoid insignificance, morally superior types continually attempt to influence others by high achievement, leadership, and martyrdom in any fashion that assures their "superiority."
3. *Control:* To avoid ridicule, controllers anticipate and control themselves and situations. They prevent the possibility of suffering embarrassment.
4. *Avoidance:* To avoid pressure and stress, avoiders function as reactors rather than actors in life. They specialize in unfinished business and unresolved problems and live as if in a temporary state.

The four priorities are present in everyone's behavioral repertoire in varying degrees. However, one of the priorities is preeminent, and the others are subordi-nated to it. The four impasse/priority concepts are regularly incorporated in

tegration centers around the person's creative development of a unified interpretation and understanding of his or her meaning and place in life. This unified understanding, which I call the *number one priority,* follows one of four general attitudes about survival (in the existential sense of having significance). These attitudes coalesce into four behavioral strategies:

1. *Pleasing:* I am meaningful and therefore can survive *only if* I am loved and appreciated.
2. *Moral superiority:* I am meaningful and therefore can survive *only if* I am better, am wiser, or know more than others.
3. *Control:* I am meaningful and therefore can survive *only if* I can control my life and the events of life that surround me.
4. *Avoidance:* I am meaningful and therefore can survive *only if* I am left alone, unpressured, and free to move.

The *only if* is perceived as an existential condition for psychic survival. It operates as if without this condition being met the person cannot go on with life. People and events in life are perceived and interpreted idiosyncratically in line with the self-selected number one priority, which, in turn, serves as a gauge for the person's reactions and behavior. The vicissitudes of life are interpreted through the private logic of the priority rather than the strict common sense of the situation. However, if the existential idea of personal identity and psychic survival is based on a narrow and fixed set of conditions, the person is less prepared for the unexpected and more susceptible to crisis.

For example, a woman deserted by her husband goes into severe crisis. Her seeming overreaction to the separation, after years of stormy marriage, abuse, and humiliation, makes no sense to her friends. The separation was both predictable and in her best interests from their perspective. However, she is

my therapeutic work and also in interviews with volunteer subjects. They help therapists understand clients quickly, and allow them to aid clients in reaching self-understanding and self-acceptance, and in recognizing the price they pay for their chosen priority and behavioral strategies.

not reacting to the immediate fact of being deserted, but to the evident proof of her conviction that "I don't have a right to exist if people don't love me." Her basic conviction and a chosen personality priority have been shattered. The separation triggered the "wrong" condition for life.

If we believe life hinges on a specific condition of existence, then the destruction of that condition results in the collapse of the world we understand and our constructs for functioning in it. Striving for balance in life means eliminating the *only ifs* and finding place and meaning in a variety of ways. The stricter the *only if* priority condition is, the more prone we are to crisis.

Previous Unresolved Disaster

A crisis can also be triggered by the recurrence of a previous unresolved traumatic experience. Let me illustrate with a real life example.

A family lost their youngest son on the first day of the Yom Kippur War in 1973. The reaction of the mother resulted in several suicide attempts, endless arguments with her family, constant crying, inability to swallow, generalized pain, and insomnia. A year earlier, it was revealed, the eldest son died of injuries in a car accident while in the army.

The mother, a self-made woman born in Morocco, had immigrated to Israel as a young woman and worked hard to get an education and develop herself. A perfectionist, she did everything in an outstanding way and overcame any obstacle in her path. Her life was exemplary in every way, including her marriage and the three accomplished children she had raised. Her life up until tragedy struck was proof to her that she could overcome any obstacle. She saw life as an uphill struggle that must be fought and won. Luck or destiny played no role in shaping it, and her accomplishments were a testament to her determination and convictions. A complete harmony existed between her value system and the life she created almost singlehandedly.

When the first son was severely injured, she was a pillar of strength, remaining at her son's bedside in the hospital for

6 months without relief to make certain he would be kept alive. The one time she was persuaded to leave and take care of urgent personal needs, he died. She buried her feelings of guilt over her absence at the end and never allowed herself to mourn his loss. Mourning, from her private logic, was perceived as a luxury. Being strong, never letting the others down, being the pillar of the family, was more important and the "right" thing for her to do. She supported the family and took care of her husband, who was severely depressed and required medication. She went on with the "business of life"—taking care of everyone else's needs.

All her efforts had a sense and a meaning. She accepted this cruel blow of life, still believing in the sacredness of the family, in togetherness as the real meaning of life, and in her power to keep the family alive and well. She handled this first loss as another feat of overcoming what life dished out. She knew life was tough and she was determined not to let it break her or the family. The unattended pain of her great loss was never addressed.

The second loss triggered a crisis. It knocked her value system apart and destroyed her faith in the future. Suddenly life was empty; nothing was left. Everything she had worked so hard to achieve was gone. Her belief system was proved wrong and she felt totally impotent. Overcome by grief and pain, she precipitously abandoned her lifelong values, making statements like, "I can't stand my family any more," "I don't want to go on living just to comfort the others," "My life is finished now, I just want to join my sons." Her "failure" to protect her sons created an intolerable sense of failure in life. The future no longer existed for her, and her automatic pilot that guided her failed once her value system had been broken.

Crisis occurs in these cases as a strong reaction, not to the immediate event alone, but as a delayed reaction to an old wound, untreated, deteriorated, and chronic.

Balance in Life and Negative Attitude to Change

A person's general attitude toward life and his or her perceived role in life also affects the predisposition to crisis. Many people idealize the desire to achieve "balance" in life by striving for a placid sea of equilibrium. Balance in life, however, is more a subject of striving than a real life description.

Apollo and Dionysus are two archetypes of Greek mythology. Apollo represents order, beauty, and harmony, while Dionysus represents passion, chaos, and the disruption of order. Apollo is calm and peaceful, ever trying to maintain tranquility, while Dionysus is ever ready to disrupt the order, to throw it off balance. In mythology, the life cycle is perceived as an alternating process with Apollo and Dionysus, in turn, taking over and dominating.

Our goal of harmony is regularly disrupted by our need to grow, learn, address problems, create, search, take risks, and strive toward the unknown. Change comes from all of these, but once established, peace and balance are needed. This alternation between Apollonian order and Dionysian disorder is not a smooth transition but full of bumps and unexpected surprises. For some, this torment is defied. Peace, harmony, and nonmovement become the ultimate condition for well-being, no matter the cost.

Change, unexpected developments, and the passing stages of life, however, cannot be avoided. To avoid them is to stop the flow of life. In reality, one can only stop oneself, not life. Becoming indifferent, not responding to stimuli, struggling to keep the order of things as they used to be then becomes the most important goal. This is a goal of maintenance rather than movement. With this sort of lifestyle, even minor change can induce a crisis.

Louis Pasteur, on his deathbed, acknowledged that a medical adversary had been right all along in insisting that disease is caused less by the germ than by the resistance of the individual invaded by the germ. The body's reaction to a germ, if "hysteric," causes crisis. Metaphorically, a crisis in mental life occurs in the same way, as a "hysteric" reaction due to a wrong interpretation of life's meaning.

When a person is in a state of crisis, one can assume that a hysteric reaction has set in. Most likely, this person has elevated the notion of balance in life to a cardinal position. When his or her sense of balance is destroyed, life becomes frightfully chaotic. Bewilderment, disbelief, rupture in values, disorientation, shock, a lack of ready responses, and a sense of time run out are characteristic of the onset of crisis.

The overwhelming fear that the situation is out of control and rapidly deteriorating compels the person to do *something*. The crisis grows in severity because the individual doesn't know what to do and becomes panicky and anxiety-ridden. Nevertheless, because the person feels compelled to make decisions, because he or she will grasp at anything to regain control, whatever actions are taken under this panic are usually counterproductive. Instead, these frenzied actions usually wind up intensifying the crisis.

Think what happens when a husband and wife use avoidance to deny a crisis looming in their relationship. Truth, anger, and pain all have to be suppressed. And what replaces the pain? More pent-up anger, more pain. As time goes by, the continued suppression of these emotions becomes progressively more difficult. Finally, a point is reached where the pain is so intolerable that one or both partners can no longer see a future. Often, it is this inability to see any future that can precipitate the onset of crisis. In a state of crisis, the victim sees *no* future, only an impending dead end, a finality, with no recourse in any direction.

Separation and divorce are the logical, almost inevitable outcome of this evolving crisis. By denying the deteriorating state of their relationship and consequently suppressing the emotions connected with it, the couple finds it necessary to avoid conflict. Each is always on guard, walking on eggs, carefully weighing every incident to avoid the impending chasm of crisis. This is the *inevitable* result. In actuality, the couple evolves from avoiding conflict to avoiding the relationship. In some relationships, which seem to survive because the couple assiduously avoids conflict situations, there is often a lingering sense of an emotional void that compels the question: What are they holding on to?

In a similar vein, we often hear people speak about a "closed person," with the implication that if the individual were somehow opened up, a wonderful treasure would be revealed. However, the opposite is generally true. A person who has been closed for many years will be *totally* empty. This is because feelings and emotions that drive the character are much like a car battery. They must be recharged by the motions and actions of life. You cannot charge up your emotional battery and then put it in storage in the garage. Feelings are recharged when we use them just as our capacities are developed by their use.

At times it is best to allow the crisis to happen. This is especially true with people whose character or lifestyle is one of long-standing avoidance. These people not only spend all their time avoiding perceived catastrophes but recruit others around them to help them achieve this.

FEAR OF THE VOID

Ernest Becker (1973), in his Pulitzer Prize winning book, *The Denial of Death,* suggests that we protect ourselves both from the inside and the outside. The inside is what Tao philosophy termed the *big emptiness* or the *big void,* something we are afraid to touch in ourselves. It is one thing to be told to "be yourself"; it is quite another to actualize this. Why is it so difficult to be our real selves? What is it we really fear? Often it is the fear that we are only a persona and a mask. We believe that there must be more to ourselves, but we harbor the suspicion that there is not.

If we could realistically perceive how small we are in relation to the cosmos, we would find it an intolerable situation. Consequently, we artificially construct a world where we can be meaningful. Our character and lifestyle are creatively fashioned by us so that we do not feel insignificant and can protect ourselves against the dreadful feeling of emptiness.

Our lifestyles are workable systems adapted to life and our place in it. The onset of a crisis always occurs when our lifestyle doesn't have the resilience to respond to the circumstances, and we are at a loss about what action to take, what guideposts to follow.

How do we know that the thing we fear and assiduously avoid is actually so bad? Our character and lifestyle are in some sense a way of looking good while covering up a cowardly interior. We are not so much afraid of bad things happening, but of discovering for ourselves and revealing to others our nothingness. In reality, nothing is stored in us. As social beings, we are, we come alive, only when we act, relate, and connect with others. As social beings, we need others to fuel and fire the spark that is within us. It is a spark that grows only when we make contact.

When the spark of connection flickers and fades, then there is only the big emptiness, which is experienced as pervasive aloneness. In crisis, people experience this intensely. Characteristically, they will say, "I have no one." Often this is untrue because friends and family members are standing by ready and willing to help. Feeling alone is an existential dimension of being. Even if there are people around trying to help, they are not perceived as such. In a crisis, the person's state of mind says, "I can't be helped."

It is difficult for the crisis worker to deal with this loneliness. Though one instinctively wants to reassure, it is useless to convince people in crisis that "You're not alone because I am with you." This feeling of loneliness is the worst part of a crisis because in this state of mind, it is actually possible to touch the big emptiness. There seems to be nothing ahead, no future, and everything that has been done in the past has failed or been cut adrift. In a state of crisis, people cannot be grateful because they cannot appreciate or even perceive what others are offering them.

IS THERE LIFE AFTER A CRISIS?

Does a crisis also offer the opportunity of a new beginning? Most people who undergo a crisis come out of it. But how is this achieved? Characteristically, when people emerge from a crisis you will find they are no longer afraid because the "worst" has indeed happened. They may now be in a state of despair, but they are no longer afraid. The first positive sign that the crisis has ended is when fear has been overcome. The person may not feel particularly courageous; he or she simply *is*. It is of course possible to resume life the way things used to be before the crisis. However, this "beyond fear" state offers one of life's rare opportunities to do things in a different way. That is why so many people embark on new beginnings—new jobs, friends, interests, and so forth.

It takes a crisis to provoke change and that is the link between crisis and change. The opportunity to change is not a reason to seek a crisis. Crisis is not beautiful, it is not poetic or heroic, and we pray we will be spared. Nevertheless, it is part of the flow of life to undergo crises, and it is certainly more normal to go through one than to spend a lifetime avoiding it.

2

Model of Crisis

In our model of crisis, three clear characteristics are always present. They are lack of information—no means to interpret the unknown, aloneness—a break in all the usual support systems, and no alternatives—a dead-end feeling.

LACK OF INFORMATION

The information void that is keenly felt in a crisis stems from a new development or radical change in a person's life. It can usually be traced either to an external event, such as a business failure, separation, disease, war, and loss of any kind, or to an inner development like depression and anxiety.

When a person's reaction to one of these is crisis, the precipitating event hits him or her suddenly, without any preparation or expectation. An old Persian proverb says that "to the blind everything happens suddenly." This saying applies to people who perceive developments in their lives as sudden, although they could have been predicted and others clearly saw them coming.

For example, after arresting a teenager, the police called the parents to notify them that their son had been charged with selling and abusing drugs. This "sudden" news triggered a crisis in the family, and the father wound up hospitalized by a heart attack. Yet, for over a year numerous clues indicated that the son's behavior was deteriorating. He was failing in school, was defiant and belligerent to his parents, had money from unknown sources, came home very late or not at all, and looked bizarre or frightening. The parents, up to a certain stage, tried to deal with these changes, but without success. Unable to communicate with him, they developed denial and helplessness and tried to cope as best they could on a superficial, everyday level. They asked questions like, "What about your exam? You don't seem to be studying for it," rather than, "Where are you spending your nights?" or "Where is all the money coming from?" which would have meant confrontation and possible solution.

They didn't confront him because they feared it might lead to a dramatic separation or disaster. Rather than face the fear, they turned to denial and "hope for better times." Clichés like "Well, adolescence is a stormy age," "He is really good at heart," and "We too were wild and difficult at this age" contributed to creating an anesthesia. When the police called on them, they found the news sudden and totally unexpected. The police call was sudden to be sure, but nonetheless predictable and only a matter of time. Fearing to interpret the implications of their son's year-long behavior meant the difference between the unknown and the expected.

Ignorant and unprepared, beset by crisis, the parents felt overwhelmed by lack of information and doubt. They were inundated by questions:

1. How should they deal with the police? Should they co-operate, which would mean giving information that might be incriminating for their son but which might

also teach him a lesson, or should they shield him no matter what?

2. Were they the guilty ones? How did they fail in his upbringing?

3. Was it his friends' influence that made him do it? Was he truly innocent?

4. If they didn't do something quickly, what would happen to him? Would he have a record for life? What should they do?

5. What if others found out? They must keep this a secret, but then who would help them?

These issues and others are legitimate questions when confronted by a difficult new situation. Normally, "new" situations are handled by applying former knowledge and experience—asking and getting advice, either from friends, experts, books, or the media. But, in the midst of the storm of crisis, it is not possible to do any of these. The usual coping mechanisms fail or seem inappropriate—and there isn't time to develop new ones before the sense of equilibrium is lost. Losing equilibrium and self-confidence also means losing trust in others, so that even if support and advice are offered, it is difficult to apply them intelligently, if at all.

Relating to Time: Past, Present, Future

In a state of crisis, sense of time is distorted. The three time frames surrounding any event or action—past, present, and future—are perceived in a new way.

Past

The past becomes the ideal time, and what the person wants more than anything else is to go back to some point in time before the "tragedy" happened. The past, a time that is now gone forever, is idealized to symbolize anything from balance to paradise. The only possible solution the person can see is to turn back the clock. He or she desperately hopes that by some miracle the event will be undone and life restored to its previous state. The dreadful feeling is that unless a replay of the event can be orchestrated, there can be no future. In extreme reactions, people *can* stop the flow of time, and, with a total lack of reality testing, cling to the past and live it again in their minds. Dalia's story is a good illustration of an extreme reaction to a tragic situation that brought on a psychotic breakdown.

Dalia's husband Danny fell in the 1973 Yom Kippur War. They were both students in their late 20s, and Danny had just begun a promising teaching career at the university. They had been married for 2 years but had known each other since their youth.

A couple of days after the official news was broken to the family, an emergency team consisting of a trained psychotherapist and a volunteer was summoned by the Ministry of Defense to make an urgent house call at the home of Danny's parents. When the team arrived, they encountered a big crowd of visitors, who had come by in the customary fashion to console and sit with the family. The father, a man in his 60s, rose to greet the team, but was stopped by Dalia, who confronted them and asked, "Who among you is the psychologist?" She looked frail and gaunt, with vacant eyes and a rigidity in her movements as though she moved without seeing what was in front of her.

As the psychologist, I accompanied Dalia to another room and asked, "How can I help you?"

She answered in a detached, unemotional way: "You see, Danny and I had decided to start a family. We fixed the date for the month of October so our child will be born next summer, right after the exams. Now that he cannot go on with his part of the plan because he died, I have to go on by myself, so that the plan will be realized. The only chance to do that on time is if I use his young brother to start immediately on the project." Not stopping for breath, still in a low voice, without emphasis, just matter-of-fact, she went on, "I considered how it should be done, whether the natural way or by artificial insemination. I prefer the natural way because there hasn't been enough experimentation yet with artificial insemination. What I need from you is help in explaining all this to his brother. I have already spoken about it, but his family doesn't seem to understand the urgency of the matter. Could you please talk to him so that we can go into the bedroom and do it? You, being a psychologist, know how to explain such things."

Dalia hadn't eaten or drunk anything for 3 days. She didn't relate to any of the visitors, didn't cry, and hardly spoke. She was obsessed with her plan, denying totally the loss of her husband. It took months of treatment for her to give up her plan and to realize that her and Danny's baby could never be. Once she could acknowledge that fact, the way was paved for her to accept Danny's death.

Future

The future is almost nonexistent for a person in a state of crisis. It exists but is constricted to the next hour or the next day. The reduction in abstract thinking that comes with crisis makes anything that is not concrete imperceivable. The future, which is an abstraction, is dreaded because the crisis victim can only anticipate that it will mean more of the same suffering he or she is presently feeling. The possibility of living in the future, beyond the crisis, is not fathomable. Therefore, no planning can take place, no motivation is active, and life is lived moment to moment. At such times, many people anticipate and welcome death because they wish this intolerable state in life to stop. This is not a suicide wish, however.

The normal flow in life needs connective tissue between past, present, and future. Once this tissue is destroyed, each of these time sequences becomes a distinct entity. The lack of connection is disorienting and emotionally alarming. The victim feels boxed in. The pain of the present can't be avoided, the idealized past becomes an unattainable dream, and the unfathomable future provokes great anxiety.

Coping on Automatic Pilot

An automatic pilot is a wonderful device that can handle complex navigational details and guide an airplane through to its destiny. However, this "pilot" has ready solutions only for those situations for which it has been programmed.

In a similar fashion, people also program themselves with

accumulated and tested solutions to life's problems. The older we get, the greater our arsenal of ready solutions and coping mechanisms for almost any development. This automatic pilot supplies us with confidence and reduces anxiety, but it can also be an obstacle to original thinking, creativity, and resourcefulness. This internalized pilot, built on past experiences, knows what is good for us and how to lead us out of whirlpools to still waters. But even the most sophisticated automatic pilot can only provide solutions to problems for which it has been programmed. Faced with a totally unexpected situation, it can't hold up for long. Faced with crisis, our automatic pilot fails and our coping mechanisms prove inadequate for lack of information.

If crisis is a disruption of balance, then the function of intervention is to help restore it by recruiting the victim's own particular coping style. In addition, after working with hundreds of bereaved people following the Yom Kippur War and observing their progress for years, we recognized an additional dimension to crisis. That dimension is to understand it as process. According to Marilyn Ferguson (1980, p. 101) in *The Aquarian Conspiracy:*

> The *importance of process* is another discovery. Goals and endpoints matter less. Learning is more urgent than storing information. Caring is better than keeping. Means *are* ends. The journey is the destination. : . . *Everything is process,* the solid world is a process. . . . A personality is a collection of processes. Fear is a process. A habit is a process. A tumor is a process. All these apparently fixed phenomena are recreated every moment, and they can be changed, reordered, transformed myriad ways.

The start of a crisis means disengaging the automatic pilot. Its absence is dreaded and the victim is desperately anxious to get back to normal life. However, if we can relate to crisis as being part of the normal processes of life, then we, as observers, can see in this "time off" period a possible transition and a potential transformation. We can then step back and allow the process to open up the possibility of new solutions, rather than rushing in to mend and restore the old automatic pilot.

From my perspective, crisis, like any other human feeling or behavior, is goal directed. Without that in mind we may fail to hear the underlying cry of the crisis victim that translates, "I cannot go on with life the way I used to." This lonely and anguished cry may signal an important stage of the process and transformation. Ironically, being forced to disengage our automatic pilot (which is the biggest fear in crisis) can lead to a new discovery of the self. That is why I suggest not regarding anxiety and panic in crisis as anything other than process. Keep that idea in mind as we turn our attention to the intervention stage.

ALONENESS—LACK OF SUPPORT

Fear and anxiety form a triangle with the sudden realization of aloneness that erupts with the onset of a crisis. Our existential condition in life is always one of being alone. It takes years of growth to reach the state of acknowledging being both whole and alone—a wholeness, a separate unity, that contains within it a complete universe. Ernest Becker (1973) speaks about "cosmic significance" and "cosmic specialness" as the ultimate goal of the child. Any child, in Becker's thinking, has within him or her all the elements needed to recreate the universe, were he or she to be the last person on earth. It is an aloneness that incorporates totality and self-sufficiency, aloneness as the unique contribution, the one that matters to the whole, or in Ferguson's (1980) words, the one that "makes the difference."

Every human being, through the socialization process, creates his or her own network or *circles of belonging*. At birth, the child becomes the center of a new circle, which expands as social development proceeds into a sequence of ever widening concentric circles of belonging. The first social circle is created between infant and mother. As the baby grows, the second circle evolves, which includes other members of the immediate family. Over time and with increasing complexity, all social relationships, including the peer group, professional group, political party, and so forth, become incorporated into the circles of belonging, where the individual remains the one and only center.

In the theory of personality priorities (Kfir, 1972; Kfir & Corsini, 1981), we regard the individual as the only holder of significance in this universe of social circles. The individual shares each circle with others, but he or she stays alone at the core of them all.

A crisis means the collapse of a person's circle of belonging. Suddenly, it no longer has meaning. The individual, who is not only the nucleus but also the connective tissue of this construct, temporarily tears the construct apart in the fall into crisis. Aloneness is then realized in a new way. The social web of a life's production only makes sense if its strands remain connected. A collapse in one important circle, if not dealt with immediately using support drawn from the other circles, results in a collapse of the total network. This is experienced as a profound aloneness, a sharp piercing sensation of an always existing truth to which we were previously numb.

We often hear the complaint of aloneness from people in crisis. In this state, they seem incapable of drawing support from others who are caring and helping. They may recognize the presence of others and may even appreciate their efforts to help, but at the same time they cannot really be reached and helped. Many people in crisis don't even remember the presence of people near them. For example:

David, at age 78, was hospitalized for the first time in his life for an operation to remove a malignant tumor. He was in a state of shock from the minute he was hospitalized, although he managed to cooperate with family and staff by turning on his automatic pilot. His recovery was very slow and he stayed in the hospital for 8 weeks, during which he also suffered numerous complications. Throughout this period, his wife stayed by him all day, and at night he had a private nurse. The few hours in between were filled by other family members and hospital staff.

After he recovered, two memories remained with David for several years: (1) the "unnecessary" operation forced on him by the panic of the family, and (2) the loneliness he had felt all that time in the hospital.

There was no way to convince him that he had never been left alone. He clung to his memory of utter loneliness and helplessness. For David, all these experiences had been sudden and alien. Helplessness and depending physically on others were totally new to him, and he wasn't able to recruit coping mechanisms for the new reality of his life. He cried out for help, and although it was given to him with love and care, he could not be reached, so overwhelmed was he by his anxiety and despair.

The sense of aloneness is like the nightmare of being left alone to face an implacable nature—storms, floods, wild animals, hunger—and crying out to family and friends, who don't respond or are nowhere to be found. There is no one. The aloneness feels like it will last an eternity. We are frail and helpless in the face of it; we are lost.

The people who are close to a person in crisis cannot see the storm or the wild animals or sense the loneliness. They are there to help, but being there does not change the crisis victim's feeling of being alone in a terrifying wilderness.

LACK OF OPTIONS

The third characteristic of crisis is the psychological state where the person cannot see any future for himself or herself, nor even the hope of having one. In relation to time, as discussed earlier in this chapter, the person focuses on the present, idealizes the past, and dreads the future. Because the individual is so overwhelmed with the present, time becomes frozen, and the present state merges with and becomes inseparable from the future. Because the present state is so unbearable and the future seems to hold no better prospect, he or she sees no solutions, no way out of the dilemma.

Crisis causes the person to regress to concrete thinking; imagery and abstract thinking do not function. The person feels he or she is going through a nightmare that cannot be stopped and that will go on forever. From that frame of mind, is generated the feeling of no choices or options.

The issue of having or not having options changes as the individual moves from stage 1 to stage 3 of a crisis.

Stages of a Crisis

Stage 1: Emotional Shock

The first reaction to a crisis-interpreted event is emotional shock. This type of shock is rarely spotted as such by the person in shock or those persons watching. The shocked person's behavior is not disturbed in a bizarre way but is inappropriate and irrelevant emotionally.

The crisis victim's interpretation of the provoking event, no matter what the source, poses such a threat to the person's existence that it seems impossible to go forward given this "nonexisting" prospect. Thus, he or she compromises with a "Scarlett O'Hara" type of reaction—"I'll think about that tomorrow." Only, unlike Scarlett's cognitive reaction, this one is due to shock. Scarlett O'Hara's reaction to catastrophe was a rather appropriate one that said, "I'll rest and let my mind work until it comes up with a solution." More importantly, her reaction meant that the situation was not critical. It could wait. She would cope.

Shock occurs when the person suffers a catastrophic loss and, unlike Scarlett O'Hara, doesn't believe that he or she can come up with a solution or that the possibility of a solution even exists. At the same time, the situation is deteriorating, out of control, and, therefore, demands a solution.

Living with the strong feeling of impending catastrophe is simply intolerable. Shock sets in as a way of detaching one's emotions from the situation.

Shock may be delayed or offset by certain circumstances. Learning about the death of a beloved throws some people into automatic pilot because they take on essential tasks such as funeral arrangements, medical and legal matters, informing others of the death and so on. Functioning at that point in time is possible in most cases so long as the focus is not on the significance of the loss.

The shock state is the organism's defense against catastrophe and collapse. It is a plea to "Let me think about it, let me get used to it, let me adapt slowly." While it is a frightening concept to most people, shock is in reality a coping defense mechanism.

In bereavement the shock state may last from 24 hours up to 6 weeks. Often, a person in this detached state is misinterpreted as "not caring," "being brave," "setting an example," and so on. Being in this zombielike emotional state is basically how the person takes care of himself or herself and prepares for the next step.

The abnormal emotional and behavioral state of a person in stage 1 is frightening to others. Intervention by family and friends at this point is generally intended to encourage the person to open up, cry, break, talk, complain, be miserable. But shock has to take its course and the pace is individual. The family fears that the person is detaching himself or herself forever, which is the reason for their intervention and demand to see the pain openly expressed.

Stage 2: Anger

In the state of shock, a person takes in information and, on a subliminal level, incubates it. By the time the person gets used to it, he or she is ready to move on. The second stage, following one of disbelief, is believing what has happened but not accepting it. The not-accepting state, unlike shock, has a fighting quality. This fighting spirit has several goals: (1) to undo the reality, and if that is not possible, (2) to fight for justice, and if that can't be attained, (3) to take revenge on others or himself or herself.

An example of undoing the reality may occur, for example, when a person learns that his or her spouse is having an affair and is leaving for good. At that point it is common for the couple to be asked by family and friends to seek marriage counseling. Typically, the counselor will find one partner to be calm, decided, beyond doubt, and difficult to reach. The other partner will fight and blame, express willingness to change in the naive hope that a reconciliation is still possible. Characteristically, this partner behaves unpredictably, moving quickly from crying to shouting to pleading, talking sense and nonsense at the same time—desperately trying to undo a situation that cannot be undone.

Accepting the finality of the loss drives the anger elsewhere. The overwhelming feeling of unfairness is predominant.

Faced with loss or deprived of the right to peaceful, undisturbed living, we feel that we didn't deserve whatever has beset us. Our Western upbringing subtly prompts our belief in law and order, in punishment and reward. What did we ever do to deserve a retarded child, cancer, a relative who is a drug addict, a desertion, the death sentence of a beloved? These questions seem appropriate since we must believe in a certain order and logic to life to find our central place in it. We want to believe with Einstein that "God doesn't play dice with the world."

So we seek an explanation. Otherwise, if there is no meaning, there may be no point in living and striving. We wind up setting out to find one reason or person to blame. We often hear people say they lost someone dear through a "foolish" death. Or they will say that car accidents are a foolish way to go. I often wonder what are the justified ways to go. Does a heroic death make it better? How many people die heroically?

Catastrophe confronts us with a blow to our basic beliefs. It jolts the contemporary mind with a harsh reminder that life is vanity, or as Shakespeare put it, "Life is a tale told by an idiot, full of sound and fury, signifying nothing."

This belief is alien to life. Viktor Frankl (1963) learned under the most brutal conditions that it was not his physical or genetic makeup that helped him survive Buchenwald concentration camp. It was his belief in the meaning of his life and his vision to tell the world about Logotherapy.

So does a sense of meaning strengthen our immune system in facing catastrophe? It can if it is strong enough, focused enough, and independent of the immediate people and circumstances. Great leaders usually possess such an intense sense, but most of us mortals need to fuel our sense of meaning with something less grandiose or ambitious. We need to nurture it with our beloved ones, our conditions of love, and a future feasible to us, one certainly not farther removed than our grandchildren's lives.

The agony of the person who experiences the unfairness of life at its most intense moment cannot be dealt with on a common-sense level. The agony must be accepted; it can't be understood.

So the anger stage is one where the person does not touch reality and cannot deal with the meaninglessness of it all.

Stage 3: Pain and Grief

In stages 1 and 2, the person is inaccessible and lost: out of touch with himself or herself in stage 1, and with others in stage 2. Moving to stage 3 is already a sign of coming back to ordinary life. However, this stage is also the longest, lasting up to a year or more. It is also the most cruel of all. It is a time when we allow reality to integrate with our being and allow the pain to surface and become part of us.

Grieving, whether expressed by tears, depression, avoidance, or other physical symptoms, offers a hopeful sign that the end of the crisis is near. Then the unfinished business will have run its course and a new beginning can occur. Allowing ourselves to grieve is a victory over the pressure that says, "What's the sense of mourning? Let bygones be bygones." It is human and right to stop the flow, to allow a breakdown to occur in order to be able to flow again.

3

Model of Intervention

For centuries, truth and wisdom about life was coveted by priests, shamans, and the elite. It remained largely unavailable to illiterate common folk, who had scant access to that wisdom, which accumulated in castles and shrines. Those truths now stare us in the face at airports, magazine stands, and bookstores everywhere, and yet we don't buy their teachings. We still cling to the belief that life is a constant flow of smooth developments. If it isn't, we remain determined to do everything in our power to make it smooth for our children, naively trusting some omnipotent being to do so. When our children suffer or are upset by life, we ask ourselves where did we go wrong?

In this age of nearly instant communication we are bombarded daily with stories of illness, tragedy, and suffering, and we are reminded that "life is pain." But, secretly, we hope that ours will not be painful. We expect to avoid pain because we are smarter, harder working, more experienced, luckier, and therefore do not deserve it. We have a tendency to separate the big promise of hope versus pain as if it were an either/or proposition. In our scenario of a good life, pain is not included. Experiencing pain and sadness is interpreted, in our Western mind set, as a disturbance rather than a natural part of the flow. In spite of all the wisdom gleaned from philosophy, religion, Eastern thinking, and especially our own experience— we still resist accepting the truth that pain, suffering, and agony are also a necessary part of life.

Pain is part of the life-stream and not a stranger that invades it. Our continued evolvement overcomes pain and uses it for processing life's unfolding material. Ernest Becker's (1973) concept of the "cosmic specialness" of the child is a specialness that, for each of us, means being able to encompass and re-create the whole cosmos just from within ourselves. The world is also desolation, conflict, destitution, and deterioration, and all of it is us.

I raise this rather somber point because it is pertinent to the goals of crisis intervention. It is not self-evident that we must always interfere with another person's life flow. Our instinctual reaction to another person's crisis, especially if that person is close to us, is an urge to stop it. That reaction stems from the goals of our own self-preservation.

Another person's crisis poses a threat to our own cherished beliefs and values. If someone dramatically and precipitously gives away all his or her worldly belongings for some noble goal, it is a crisis we cannot tolerate. It challenges our own need for property and makes fools of us.

When a person tries to kill himself or herself, we pause and momentarily question our own tight hold on life. When a person seems to give up a stable marriage, job, or country, our own foundations are a bit shaken as we confront the possibility that our beliefs, our "truths," are not necessarily so.

The reaction to crisis is very often along the lines of "it must be stopped before. . . ." Nonetheless, unless we are ready to accept crisis as a normal part of the flow of life, we are ill equipped to know how to intervene. We must recognize courage in a person who enters into crisis and allows himself or herself "time out" to experience the dead end. Working through a crisis is like growing; it is done alone. Some babies rise in the morning, and, behold, the new tooth is there, an easy gift. Others suffer high temperatures, irritability, and sickness before each tooth emerges.

On the other hand, don't forget for 1 minute how frightening and unheroic a crisis is. We do not choose to be in crisis. We simply choose to let go, to let it be. Our automatic pilot goes on functioning, but our self stops its flow for a while. Marilyn Ferguson's (1980) metaphor of the pendulum is helpful. In crisis our pendulum goes mad, swinging wildly at an accelerated pace, but it is still connected to its rod, and eventually it will return to its steady pace.

Crisis means a change in the flow of life. The river flows relentlessly to the sea. When it reaches a point where it is blocked by rocks and debris, it struggles to find ways to continue its path. Would the alternative be to flow backward? That is what a person in crisis craves, to go back in time. But life doesn't provide a reverse gear, and the struggle must go forward, like the river, with occasional pauses to tread water and check out where we are heading.

INTERVENER VERSUS INTERVENTION

It is important to differentiate the goals of the intervener from the goals of intervention. Interveners want to correct and harmonize, stop the storm and struggle, and make the world calm again. Being with a person in crisis is being in crisis. Professional detachment has nothing to do with being part of the crisis. It takes courage and understanding to allow ourselves to really be there, to enter the turbulence. We, as interveners, are frightened, not because we don't understand what is taking place. We are terrified because we know deep inside exactly what it is all about. So we pretend we don't understand, declining to accept that the person has gone astray. We deny the other's protest and will to struggle, presenting ourselves as being supportive while actually trying to stop a process of change and potential growth.

Crisis and change can be twin brothers if we allow them.

The goals of intervention, not of the intervener, are to see a person through the process, to offer advice, to open the sluice gates so the flow can go forward. The fear of crisis and the fear of change are rooted in our need for balance. Apollo and Dionysus are once again pulling us in two directions.

LEVELS OF INTERVENTION

The model of intervention is based on the model of crisis described earlier. The people who serve as crisis interveners can include family, friends, volunteer laypersons, or professionals (social workers, therapists, doctors, and healers of all kinds). Training laypersons for intervention is widely practiced today. Often they run the crisis centers under professional supervision.

In other respects, crisis intervention differs from usual forms of psychotherapy. Crisis intervention focuses on the present alone. It relates primarily to the situation, or rather the person in that situation, and not on the personality or personal history. The intervention is direct, and the intervener controls the session. He or she must be trustworthy, authoritative, and knowledgeable and must regard the intervention as a short encounter, possibly a one-time occurrence, as that is often all that is possible. The goals of the intervention must be immediate, concrete, and feasible.

Intervention occurs on three levels: giving information; providing support by involvement, moral or practical; and providing alternatives and immediate concrete activities.

Giving Information

When crisis strikes it brings on a feeling of reaching a dead end because it looms up suddenly as an unknown void and offers no guideposts to follow. It is a situation filled with anxiety, giving the crisis victim a feeling of impending catastrophe, no sense of a future, and no idea how to proceed. The frightening unknown during a crisis does not concern the mysteries of life, but what to do in the next hour. Giving information is invaluable at this stage. The term *information* is used instead of *awareness* or *consciousness* for a purpose. Simple, concrete information is better suited to the needs of a person in a crisis state with the characteristically diminished ability to abstract, assess, remember, or grasp the total picture.

The goal of giving information is to reduce anxiety and connect the private (idiosyncratic) logic of the person in light of what has happened to the common sense of ordinary life. By doing this we help pull him or her out of the pit toward the rest of us. Such information should be correlated with the person's ability to absorb it. It should neither tire nor alarm. Rather, it should be simple, direct, practical, and usable. Three levels of information can be used depending on the person's state of being and his ability to absorb: referral information about available services—communication and help; information about similar kinds of situations—norms and standards; and professional feedback, that is, information gleaned from our assessment of what the person is undergoing, how long it can be expected to last, and what can be expected from the process.

Information about Available Services—Communication and Help

The following example best illustrates this level of information:

A man, 28 years old, was brought to our Maagalim Crisis Center. He had arrived in Israel some 2 months earlier, a newcomer from England. He had no command of Hebrew and knew little of life in this country. A professional chef, he found work very quickly at one of the hotels. After 1 week on the job, he accidentally severed his thumb on a bread-cutting machine. He received first aid at a hospital emergency unit and was released. Then the signs of panic set in. With 2 months rent already due, no means to pay it, and the inability to continue working, he moved into the street and slept in the park. Cold and hungry, alone, not knowing which way to turn, he was overtaken by anxiety. He believed that he was dying of blood loss and gangrene. He was brought to our center by a man who found him in the park in the throes of a severe anxiety attack.

To help him, our center gave him several levels of information. He was told where to go for temporary lodging, how to follow up the surgery on his thumb, the rights of new immigrants in an emergency, social security rules, and so on. A volunteer escorted him to the various locations for these services. By the end of the day, he had a room at an absorption center, his injury was treated and redressed, and he was given a small sum of money to provide for his needs. He was also invited to return to the center the following week.

Assessment information was also given. His state of shock and need for a recovery period of absolute rest for a week was explained. He was not referred to his parents in England at his request. We did refer him to various appropriate services where further help could be found. Reorientation and future life planning information, now that he could no longer work as a chef, were delayed with the promise to deal with them at a later stage.

Information and referral were suggested and carried out as the first step. At that stage, he was so anxiety-ridden he had no way of helping himself. Unless and until the most pressing issues of his health and well-being were treated, he would head nowhere. His crisis was triggered by a sudden extreme situation. Because he was totally unequipped, already in the midst of another big change in life (immigration), and separated from his family, the loss of job and a place to stay was more than he could handle. He would probably have coped satisfactorily on his own had this event happened a year later, or a year earlier at home in England. In light of the "fight or flight" paradigm, he chose flight. Intervention removed that stark choice, and allowed him to flow through the situation and resume his life.

Information about Similar Situations—Norms and Standards

Another form of information is the exposure to knowledge about similar situations, the norms, procedures, and possible outcomes of the process.

The person in crisis operates in a heightened state of awareness and is eager to be informed about his or her situation. The sense of losing control, of facing the unknown, of behaving differently than normal, leads to the belief that he or she is becoming insane. This feeling exacerbates the critical state and forces the person to act in an effort to stop it. But the action that results is usually poorly directed and drives the person to compound the panic.

Valid information from an authoritative source is not only helpful; it can eliminate the panic and encourage the person to accept what is going on with less anxiety or even remove anxiety all together.

For example, Zippi, age 31, came by herself to our crisis center from a small town in northern Israel. She was skinny, tiny, pale—looking half her age. The mother of two boys, ages 4 and 6, she was recently divorced, had her own apartment (provided by social security), and a pension. She told us she was extremely depressed for several months since her divorce. She was spending most of the day in bed, unable to eat or sleep, feeling chest pains, and wanting to die. Unable to care for her sons, she consequently felt very guilty. Yet at the same time she wished that they would be taken away.

Her short history went as follows. She was married at 22 to a man prone to violence and all manner of addiction. He beat her regularly and brutally, and he beat the children as well. After the second child arrived, she mounted the courage to fight back and saved herself and the children. She spent a couple of years in and out of shelters, courts, social agencies, and received plenty of help and sympathy. Finally, she succeeded in getting her divorce and custody of the children.

All those long years she lived in poverty. Alone, under constant threat, she maintained a fighting spirit, was self-encouraged, and proceeded with a clear goal in mind. She didn't mind the hardships as long as the hope of regaining her freedom and rebuilding her life sustained her. After her long and painfully awaited divorce was decreed, she reached the victory of freedom and security. But at the same time, she "lost" her big goal, and with it, her hope and fighting spirit. The long repressed fatigue and mourning for her young life took over. All of these factors coalesced and depression overtook her. She became fearful, anxiety-ridden, and suspicious of everything that was happening to her and questioned whether she was going out of her mind. She had no way of understanding this reaction, so it only fed her despair, impotence, and wish to die. Being consumed for so long with only one hope and goal, she now found herself without either and with no sense of the future. She was totally unprepared for the future. Her future had always been the day of divorce, not the morning after.

A similar phenomenon occurred after people were liberated from the concentration camps. There were those who by sheer force of will survived and clung to life through their hope alone. Once they realized they had actually survived, they found themselves without a goal. They had no vision of a future beyond survival and lost hope. That explains why many of them, overtaken by an unfathomable, empty future and an unbearable fatigue, killed themselves.

The information given to Zippi was designed to assure her that her reaction was normal. This contrasted sharply to the perplexed "why now?" reaction of friends who couldn't understand her sudden change in behavior. She was given examples of others who had had similar experiences. She was told that she was undergoing a normal process that would take its course, that there was a need for mourning and its accompanying depression, and that recharging and change would come later.

Cognitive information, even in times of crisis, is stored and will be processed later on. The main goal is to reassure the client he or she is "normal," and that what he or she is experiencing is part of a process that sorts itself out for the better and not for the worse.

Providing Support by Involvement, Moral or Practical

The aloneness of a person in crisis calls for support, and his or her despair provokes one to intervene and help. The help and support offered cannot stop the sense of aloneness discussed earlier, but they are needed to ease the path to recovery.

The support works like hidden footholds in a sheer canyon wall; once found they provide a step-by-step passage to safety. Support also works like an echo of reality and provides assurance that one is still in touch with it. It is also paradoxical in that it is most needed when one's behavior seems least deserving. When crisis pushes one to behave poorly, to be irresponsible, withdrawn, and alienated, support says the world is still there, and offers a bonus—"You're OK"—which is especially needed at this time.

This discussion may appear self-evident from the perspective of those with professional background and training, but being self-evident doesn't minimize its importance. To emphasize its value, I've adopted some insights on support from *A Course in Miracles* (Singh, 1986), which deals with "miracles" that happen in everyday life. By substituting the word *help* for *miracles*, we can derive some uncommon statements about help:

1. There is no order of difficulty in help. One form is not harder than another. They are all the same. All expressions of love and care are maximal.
2. Help is mutual; when it doesn't occur, something has gone wrong.
3. Help is everyone's right.
4. Help is an exchange.
5. Help bears witness to truth; it is convincing when it arises from conviction.
6. Help is a teaching device; it simultaneously strengthens the giver and the recipient.
7. Help is the maximum service you can render to another.
8. Help depends on cooperation.
9. Help is a natural sign of forgiveness.
10. Help should inspire gratitude, not awe.
11. Help is never lost.

Any involvement is support, whether through practical actions, giving guidance, taking over obligations, providing physical caretaking, or just being there. It was this realization that opened the way for our structured social institutions to enlist laypersons and volunteers to offer support. The inadequacy of our institutions to deal with persons in crisis has encouraged more and more people from all walks of life to step in and offer assistance. Training laypeople for this kind of intervention is the big and rewarding social task ahead of us.

To understand the diversity of ways support can be needed and given, consider two biblical figures who suffered tragedies, Job and King David. Job's tragedies were monumental and included the loss of his family and fortune and his bout with leprosy. In the face of these big losses he despaired. He could not go on with life unless he understood why those things happened to him.

King David likewise suffered greatly. Persecuted by King Saul for years, he fled into the desert. He lost his baby for his sins, lost his most beloved son, Absalom, who led the mob against him, had to give up his dream of rebuilding the Temple as a punishment for the bloodshed, and, in the end, lost his best friend, Jonathan. In spite of all that, David was never in crisis. He did not ask God for explanations. He took what life dished out to him and went on with living.

Job's three friends sat with him, gave information and explanations, assisted, urged, and demanded Job's recovery. Job ignored their help and pleaded to God to intervene. Only the divine would be an acceptable source of answers. Nevertheless, his friends didn't leave him, nor did they feel insignificant even though their advice was not heeded.

David, throughout his life, found comfort in the assistance Jonathan gave from a distance. The Bible doesn't tell much about this assistance, but it was there, a reality in the minds of the two friends.

These classic stories illustrate the point that different people need different kinds of help and that there is no one way of giving support or intervention.

Providing Alternatives and Immediate Concrete Activities

The despair over a perceived lack of alternatives and reaching a dead end is a sign of the person's own assessment of his crisis. Beyond information and support, intervention must deal, in the end, with alternatives.

This concept may sound too ambitious to many crisis

workers. We know that people in crisis are generally fixed on only one solution—to restore what existed before the crisis. But this is the one solution we cannot offer. Consequently, it frequently leads to a feeling of helplessness on our part. Sometimes we feel that unless we can undo the crisis or its cause, we fail to really help. This model challenges that attitude. Life, as long as it goes on, means alternatives. They exist even when we cannot see them. Crisis is a case in point. Alternatives don't mean solutions, but a way out, one step forward, one step at a time.

If we look at the situation in terms of left and right brain functions, the person in crisis is unable to assess, imagine, or see any chance of solution. The inventive spirit, needed more than ever in times of crisis, is immobilized. That is why intervention by others who can use right brain assessment and see alternatives can be so crucial. Bear in mind, however, I am not suggesting big breakthroughs, happy endings, or miracles, but only the idea of a step at a time. To be effective, we must stay out of the person's arena of crisis and yet be identified as the one who knows what can be done.

Alternatives that can be offered might include the following:

1. *Homework:* any activity—even resting can be perceived as an activity. The activity should evoke immediate relief, mental or physical. It should be of short duration, at maximum a week. Emphasis should be placed on doing the activity, not its outcome.
2. *Enabling:* introducing control in the situation by authoritative assignments, actions, and supervision.

The objective is to focus on these activities and not at all on the subject of crisis. For example, a young woman came to the crisis center with a 5-month-old baby, her first. She had been married for 2 years. Her father was dying of cancer in the hospital and her mother was confined at home recovering from a heart attack. Her brothers and sisters, for different reasons, didn't visit either parent and remained unmoved by the family drama. One had a shop to tend, another lived far away, one was in the army, and one had a hospital phobia. She alone was left to take care of both parents. She visited her father every day, baby in hand, and returned home, after traveling on two buses, exhausted, depressed, and feeling hopeless. She was indifferent to the baby, to housework, and to her husband. She felt alone and deserted, and stress had taken its toll physically. She was driving herself toward collapse.

She came to the center seeking advice about her marriage. Her husband threatened to leave her if she didn't stop the daily visits to the hospital and resume taking care of herself, the baby, and him. She felt trapped. She couldn't neglect her dying father, nor could she make her brothers and sisters help, and she couldn't let her marriage collapse. She saw no solution to the dilemma she faced. No matter what change she might make, she'd suffer a devastating blow, separation, guilt, or impotence.

The staff of the center couldn't see an immediate solution to her dead-end dilemma either. Their primary concern was getting this young woman to the point where she could handle the situation from a position of strength and freedom. After reviewing her situation with her, the staff offered the following alternatives:

1. For the next week, and only for 1 week, she would visit her father only three times.
2. The other days of the week would be devoted to resting, eating, and getting outdoors.
3. For the next day, her best friend would be requested to take care of the baby so she could spend the whole day in bed. She was encouraged to call her friend from the center and ask her help.
4. She would inform her father today about the upcoming week's schedule.
5. To avoid strife, she was not to ask her siblings for help nor to inform them of her plan.
6. She was reassured that in a week she would be better able to proceed.

7. She was told to call the center daily and return 1 week later.
8. She was "commanded" not to deal with housework, but to concentrate on her own needs.
9. She was asked to report to her husband what was suggested and request that he join her the following week at the center.

These instructions and suggestions gave her immediate relief. She felt in control, supported, and that her actions and behavior were OK since they had been "authorized" by experts. Furthermore, she was relieved not to have to deal with problems of family cooperation from her siblings or husband for the entire week.

HOLISTIC APPROACH TO CRISIS

Although we regard crisis as caused mainly by our mental and psychological interpretation of a given situation, we must not neglect the fact that our total being, soul and body, experiences it together.

Behavior Patterns in Crisis

Although there is no specific mode of behavior that all people follow in crisis, there are observable patterns and characteristic symptoms. These symptoms fall into three main categories: the physical, the mental, and the social.

Physical Changes

The most common reactions are headaches, but a wide variety of symptoms are likely, including lack of appetite, insomnia, inability to swallow, chest pains, rapid heartbeat, skin rashes, and so on.

Mental Changes

People in a state of crisis lose much of their ability to concentrate or focus their thinking. They tend to repeat themselves, forgetting what they have already said. There is a difficulty in differentiating between the essential and the irrelevant. Words get lost, and what is meant to be said can't be recalled when needed. They suffer from fatigue and at the same time the awareness of pressure and urgency. They sense that they are not dealing properly with an urgent situation but don't know what to do.

Social Changes

A normal, interactive social life is reduced to a minimum or none at all for the crisis-ridden person. The content of relationships is limited to functional issues. Others, even significant others, are only perceived remotely and temporarily lose their special significance. Others can serve as listeners, but there won't be an investment in the relationship by the person. This explains the common experience of "losing" one's friends in times of crisis. The person in crisis needs all his or her energy just to maintain existence, and none is left for anyone else.

Over the years we discovered that what is called the wisdom of the desert, an anonymous concept, can be extremely helpful in crisis situations. It relates to the power of distraction. When we have a pressing issue to solve and are unable to find a solution by thinking it through, we can try any of the following: meditation, prayer, relaxation, sleep—symbolically retreating to the desert. This distraction, at first glance, seems a loss of precious time. But allowing ourselves to retreat shows that our minds do supply us with solutions, often quite unexpectedly. Many people don't realize that physical training can be a desert and can serve the same goals of distraction and energizing.

Putting a crisis- or stress-ridden person on a short-term regimen of diet and exercise has proven to be very helpful. Consequently, we stress this point with three kinds of homework. Whenever possible, we try to enlist a supporter to help the crisis victim perform the assignments. Generally, we ask the person in the crisis to invite a relative or friend to go through the homework program with him or her.

We suggest either a 3-day or 1-week program of (1) dieting or fasting, (2) brisk walks once or twice a day, and (3) hot and cold showers done successively in the morning followed by deep breathing.

By fasting we mean a monodiet, based on fruits and juices. We recommend 3 days of watermelon, apples, or grapes during which the person can eat as much as he or she wishes. (We generally provide some recommended reading on the subject to help the individual understand the diet's function.) Slightly less rigorous than the monodiet would be 3 days of light eating based on fresh fruits and vegetables.

The walks are a feasible task that encourages blood circulation, provides fresh air and invigorated breathing, and boosts morale. The showers, if carried out as suggested, induce movement, shouting, cold water reaction, and laughter (especially if done with a supporting partner). Deep breathing techniques are taught and practiced at the intervention session.

These options are inexpensive and feasible. They provide an immediate sense of control, a sense of purpose and achievement, and, for many, a new aspect of life.

Interveners, while undergoing training, learn about the roles of food, exercise, and relaxation for the first time. Yet they are often reluctant or embarrassed to suggest such "simple" advice when the person before them has just lost a beloved, a business, or is otherwise anxiety-ridden.

This is what we mean by *options*. We do not suggest another love, another business, or to a young woman who has just miscarried, "You are young; you'll have other babies." Common-sense suggestions are unnecessary mainly because they will happen anyhow as life takes its course. What is desperately needed at this point is something that can be done right away to help the person restore control, have a goal, and feel a sense of pride and achievement. It should provide a temporary distraction, a preoccupation with a new subject that is far removed from the crisis-causing trouble.

We used the verb *suggest,* but often that is not enough in crisis intervention. We have to help *make* the person do it. Kind, sympathetic suggestions by interveners often fail to get people to follow the plan. As mentioned earlier, authoritativeness is extremely important since the person in crisis has lost trust in his or her own authority and sense of direction. Another person must provide these for him or her. *Authority* in this context means knowledge, experience, caring, and the patience of a midwife to see the person through the crisis.

Information giving depends on our knowledge and ability to communicate it. Support depends on how much time and commitment we have. Options are just there. It is our task, more than offering comfort or sympathy, to tell individuals facing crisis what they can do for themselves. These are the options. If the person in crisis puts them to use, new energy can start flowing, and crisis may turn into change.

CRISIS AND CHANGE

I was asked a question some time ago that I misunderstood. The question was "How can you deal all the time with people undergoing crisis?" My understanding of the question was "How can you tolerate all that pain?" But the inquiring person corrected me by saying, "I didn't mean the pain, I meant how do you tolerate so many people making major changes after undergoing crises? Doesn't it make you feel like you're missing out, and that you wish for a crisis?"

Indeed, people beyond fear, in the nothing to lose state that often follows a crisis, can see a new dimension. Once the paradigm breaks, people are free to choose new directions. Knowing more, people often change after a crisis. It may be an actual move to another home, a new car, new colors in the home, new vocation, friends, political stands, and interests. Some discover painting, writing, traveling, exercise, and possibly love. If Jampolsky (1979) is right in saying "Love is letting go of fear," then at that critical point in life we have just that chance.

Real change is often started from the depths of the pit of despair. As long as we interveners remember that, our counselees have genuine hope.

II

CASE STUDIES

In the second part of the London workshop we worked with several people who were invited by their doctors and psychotherapists. These volunteers were in therapy or medical treatment, and their therapists believed them to be in crisis or imminently facing one.

These people knew ahead of the session that they were going to be counseled in front of a group of therapists and that the audience would be involved. This is the way we teach, with the client as part of the group rather than by being observed through a one-way mirror or being discussed in absentia. Live supervision offers three advantages—ones for the client, the therapist, and the learners or group.

CLIENT'S ADVANTAGE

The person who is counseled gets immediate support from the group. The group setting provides an opportunity to discuss values, taboos, and secrets. Through the group interaction, the client is informed and reassured that others in the room share his or her problems and concerns. This in itself is supportive. During our workshop, numerous people offered to share their own private logic about issues like masturbation, homosexuality, jealousy, going mad, hating one's own child, and the fear of dying. We were able to discuss these issues, and in so doing give the client new information and legitimize certain feelings, which in itself relieves anxiety.

The power of the group extends beyond support. The concentrated thinking and concern of the group, the focused attention, and the greater accountability the client feels in front of a group add greatly to the impact of the session. In addition, the heightened awareness that words count, the time allowed for reflection, and the strong desire for the session to be useful within the time constraints posed contribute to the impact of the group.

THERAPIST'S ADVANTAGE

For therapists, live supervision may seem threatening in the beginning. Nevertheless, it offers several possibilities for a breakthrough in the therapy. First, there is the value gained by the variety of feedback about the client's situation and alternative possibilities. Second, seeing the client through the eyes of one's colleagues is a learning experience. Third, a self-exposure comes from sharing one's ideas and asking for help and enlightenment.

Therapists are interveners, and in that role, they also need intervention. The therapist as well as the client gets encouragement and support, in addition to sympathy for the difficulty of the case and respect for the responsibility and exposure. In modeling and shaping the request for advice, the therapist makes the whole issue of therapy an equal project.

GROUP'S ADVANTAGE

For learners, future therapists, and those already in practice, the live supervision provides the opportunity to see how it is really done. Every learner in the session is not just an observer, but also a participant in the responsibility for what is taking place. Group members may interrupt, ask questions, and try out ideas.

It is important that the group never refers its questions or points directly to the counselee, but to the supervisor. The reason for this is to protect the person from those questions or hypotheses that might increase stress. The supervisor channels the group's questions or comments to the counselee. Therapy, or intervention, is a process of constant decision making and assessment. Unless one has the opportunity to observe and be part of the process, it is difficult to learn.

The supervisor uses the group setting for co-counseling. Referring to the group gives the counselee a break and the opportunity to also be an observer. More than that, the therapist can confront the client through talking to the group and can raise ideas to which the client does not have to respond, only listen and assess.

In this workshop, there was a need to enlarge on topics that came up that were pertinent but not necessarily directly related to the client's situation. Good examples would be the whole issue of normal and abnormal behavior, being in control versus being out of control (going mad). Generalized discussion takes the pressure off, enhances learning, and promotes changing attitudes toward the subject at hand. We tried with all the counselees at this workshop series to provide a new supply of information, general support, and some options in line with general actions and practical homework. Of course, these options varied depending on whether we were treating anxiety, problems in a relationship, bereavement, or psychological problems associated with terminal cancer.

Interveners are often hesitant when they meet people with terminal diseases. Much like friends and family, the intervener takes it on himself or herself to supply hope for life. If this cannot be done sincerely, it shouldn't be done. Interveners must relate to the real situation, help the client realize whatever is available, not simply what is wished. In the session with Richard and Susan (Chapter 9), Richard said that he wanted to be happy and not worry all the time about his cancer spreading. We tried to deal with reality. Can a person be happy at that stage? We tried out other possibilities for him to consider like faith, friends, and writing. These are options that focus on what he can do for himself and by himself, rather than an outcome or byproduct such as happiness that cannot be reached directly.

Throughout the workshop, we used exercises to make certain points even stronger. Mostly, the exercises were offered to help persons feel their own strength, or locked up energy and unused power, and to experience using it.

The need of persons in crisis to repeat their story with detailed dates, places, and events is satisfied by the patient listening of the group, their feedback, and the limits set by the supervisor.

All the sessions in the following chapters would be classed as one-time interventions. Follow-up was provided by the patient's doctor or therapist. Some of the sessions ended with a discussion, others didn't need it, and a few left us beyond speech—with no words suitable to express the deep feelings that welled up in our hearts.

4

Brian: Control in the Face of the Uncontrollable

INTRODUCTION

This section opens with Brian because he is the only person who used our workshop as a crisis intervention center. Brian reached a critical breaking point the previous evening and was anxious to get help because he was alarmed at what was happening to him. Since he was not in therapy, this session illustrates a one-time intervention, with possibly no follow-up and with no supportive therapist. We had to fulfill all intervention goals in one session. It began with an introduction of Brian to the group by a friend, who happened to be a therapist attending the workshop.

SESSION DIALOGUE

Therapist: Brian owns the gym where I work out. I went there this morning to lift some weights and was met by Brian's business partner, whose first words were, "Hi, did you hear about Brian?" And, of course, I hadn't. He explained what had taken place the previous Friday, and it became clear to me that Brian was in crisis. I asked him if he was prepared to come this evening, and this he agreed to do.

Nira: Brian, can you tell us about the situation you find yourself in?

Brian: On Friday evening, I was called by my mother, who was in a very distressed state. She is blind, diabetic, and in the past 4 months has had three serious heart attacks. She is 67 years old, very bright, and very dominant. My father, on the other hand, is introverted, tall, and deaf. Generally, they get on okay and have a pretty good time. At the age of 31, I am beginning to discover them and am building a friendship with them both. The reason for my mother's distressed phone call was that a taxi had dropped my father at the end of the drive in a very inebriated state. The best thing my mother could do was let him sleep it off. I arrived home at about 12:30 A.M. to discover that he had in fact had a stroke. I called an ambulance, and within a short time he was in a hospital. My sister, who lives in the Midlands and has a 9-month-old baby, arrived on Saturday. Things were sorting themselves out pretty well until my mother suffered another heart attack and was taken to a different hospital.

I am finding it very hard to cope. The onus is on me to help as much as I can because my sister has a baby and lives about 100 miles away. At first I thought it was simply a matter of getting the house sorted out. I know that I appear to be concerned very much with organizational matters, but at the moment this is simply how I perceive things. I pride myself on being very calm and collected. But last night I simply went to pieces. I brought my mother's guide dog up in my father's car and my father, not liking dogs, had a go at me. I lost my temper, threw things and slammed doors. Afterward, I felt very foolish and now feel confused. I don't know what to do or where to go. Much of the time, I am on the verge of tears. I am not used to feeling this way, and find it difficult. At the moment, any decision, either business or otherwise, has become almost impossible to make. I oscillated for the whole day on whether or not to come this evening.

Nira: I take it this is not the way you usually handle decisions.

Brian: I am normally decisive, and now I am lost.

Nira: Have you ever been in a situation that has any similarity with this one?

Brian: In all honesty, I haven't . . . except perhaps when my mother started to have heart attacks and was taken to the hospital last November. However, in many ways, that was easier to cope with. It was only one parent, and the responsibility did not fall completely on my shoulders.

Nira: I would like, first of all, to try to describe the kind of situation that you are in. What you have been describing is a situation of crisis. In what way is it different from other stresses you have undergone in your life? First of all, it is a completely new situation, one for which you do not have ready responses. A great deal of what you are currently going through is unknown. You also have a total responsibility because your parents can't communicate. Nothing in your past experience gives you any clue about what is going to happen. You have some ideas about what will happen, and some of these you are finding difficult to take. Here, I would like to say something to the group.

[To the group:] Brian has told us that his parents have been limited for quite some time. What I am about to say may seem to some extent paradoxical, but if you live with people who have limitations, you become used to these limits and feel these individuals can overcome anything. It is when these people go through a real catastrophe that you begin to lose confidence. We have seen that Brian is a person who generally copes well with situations. Here, as he has explained, he is confronted by something that is completely new.

[To Brian:] Are you a person who inspires trust, and do your parents trust you?

Brian: Yes, I suppose that I do inspire trust, and I think that my parents have begun to trust me now. I was at boarding school from about the age of 9 to the age of 16. From then

until the age of 24, there was an enormous hostility between me and my parents, so much that I left home and
went to London. It is only now that we have really started
to relate well to each other.

Nira: Have you changed roles in the last couple of years? Have
you become their parent?

Brian: Very much so. Without wishing to slight them in any
way, I have never seen them as having much of a parental
role for me. Even when I was a child, my father and I were
very different; I am very practical, and he is an austere
academic who is very noncommunicative. I don't think he
understands me at all.

Nira: So you have changed roles; now you are the parent.

Brian: That is a very easy role to assume because I am a bossy
and dogmatic person by nature. I used to push them into
making decisions, and now I have to learn how to pull back
a bit.

Nira: Before you came here this evening, we were discussing
the question of self-awareness. You have given us a great
deal of basically positive information about yourself. Nonetheless, you have put it over in a negative way. Is there
anything positive that you could tell us about yourself?

Brian: I find this very difficult.

Nira: Sell yourself.

Brian: Deep down, I have a very low self-image and find it
extremely difficult to accept affection, friendship, or praise.

Nira: I actually asked for positive statements and facts, not
images.

Brian: I am bright, perceptive, honest, and kind to people. I
do not generally "damage" people, less at any rate than I
see people around me doing. I am happy, I enjoy life, and
I am good at organizing things. I take charge of my own
life, and I give it a direction. I have great discipline over
the things that I want, and none over the things that should
be important.

Nira: It is interesting that you have used the word *organization*
so often today. You have basically described the situation
with which you are faced as an organizational one and
have said that you are good at organizing things. Does this

connect in any way with you? [To the group:] Here is a person who is good at organization. The crisis he is facing is largely organizational. How can this be understood?

Group: What has affected him has been much deeper than simply at an organizational level.

Nira: Are you saying that you can be good at organization as long as your emotions are not involved?

Group: Although Brian is in a crisis, to a large extent he is in control of the situation.

Nira: Yes, but what we are trying to ascertain is why a person in his situation feels totally out of balance. Although it probably did him some good, why did he have this fit in his flat last night? He keeps on mentioning the word *organization,* and I think that it connects.

Group: Perhaps organization has something to do with being able to control the situation? Currently he is unsure about what will happen and is therefore unable to control it.

Nira: Let us see if we can make a connection in another way and, Brian, I will try to use your own words. You said you try not to "damage" people. I would like to check this with you because it seems that perhaps this is at the heart of the matter. If you don't take correct action and make correct decisions, you may do damage. Could this be a very frightening prospect?

Brian: I have to say that the comment about control is perhaps the more pertinent one. I am fully aware that I have a need to control my environment because it removes the uncertainty. It is this more than anything that causes my problem now. Because I don't know what is going to happen with my parents, it is out of my control. Because of what I do and what I have, I know that I organize things very well. However, it is the result of my rigid control, and over the past year it has been a great strain for me. The worst feeling that I can have is one of helplessness.

Group: What does helplessness mean to you? Does it mean that you can be damaged?

Brian: I don't think it is as simple as that. Helplessness in me produces an almost phobic reaction. I will rush around in a frantic state to regain control.

Nira: At any time in your life do you remember being helpless?
Brian: No.
Nira: Were you a healthy child?
Brian: Yes.
Nira: All the time?
Brian: Yes.
Nira: What about your family?
Brian: Yes, with the exception of my mother, who has been diabetic for many years. When I was a child, whenever she went into a diabetic coma, it was always I who swung into action. My father wouldn't have known what to do.
Nira: Did you see your father as a helpless and impotent person?
Brian: I still do. I used to be infuriated at his inability to do things. I think that now I understand it.
Nira: You accept it, I don't know whether you understand it.
Brian: He is hopelessly impractical and very, very incapable. I find myself taking things from him.
Nira: You mean his role?
Brian: I don't see him as having a role as such. Although she always maintains that it is my father who has the last word, it is my mother who has always made the decisions in the house.
Nira: Can you accept her authority?
Brian: Pragmatically, I must have rebelled against it because when I was 16 they had expectations about what I was going to do and what I was going to be. I reacted by leaving home. I became a petrol pump attendant and lived in a grotty flat in London. This didn't exactly fulfill their aspirations. In the long term, I did everything opposite from that which they had wished.
Nira: Do you feel you have enough information about their situation or what is going on in these hospitals? Do you trust them?
Brian: I trust as long as I have enough information and can input something. I am the type of person who will phone, visit, pester, and push until I have all the facts.
Nira: Do you have all the facts now?
Brian: Yes.

Nira: Let us deal with each family member separately. What is your father's situation at the moment?

Brian: He has had a dense CVA, hemiplegia, and has lost the use of his left leg, although he has retained use of his left arm. He is 63 years old, young for a stroke victim. He has also lost the use of the left side of his face, and his speech is impaired; half the vision in his left eye has also gone. He will probably stay in the hospital for about a month. I was a social worker for 7 years and I also worked in Park Three Homes for 3 years. I had quite a lot of experience working with the elderly, especially stroke victims. One of the most difficult things I have to come to terms with is knowing what Park Three Homes are like. It gives me goose pimples just thinking about it. I would find it very hard to deal with the guilt if I allowed one of my parents to enter such an institution.

Nira: But let us look at the short-term future. In about a month, your father will come out of the hospital. What will happen at that time? When he comes home, your mother will not be there. Who will be at home?

Brian: Nobody.

Nira: So how can you deal with this?

Brian: I am dealing with it in the best way that I am able. I have pestered the life out of the medical social workers at the hospital to provide meals on wheels and a district nurse to visit (which I know my father will hate). But it is just not adequate.

Nira [to the group]: How many of you know people in a similar situation who have lived alone and taken care of themselves?

Group: I knew someone in her late 60s who had a stroke and lived for a very long time.

Nira: How did she handle this?

Group: In the fashion that she had always existed, and therefore she could cope. But I think that generally this is unusual.

Group: I know of a woman, 89, who lives alone and is confined to a wheelchair. She has a shrill whistle. Anyone who passes knows that if they hear it she needs some assistance.

Brian: I am currently organizing a pendant for my father. If you press it, it dials through to a main computer and calls an emergency service. I have already contacted the local Round Table about this. In other respects, how will my father cope? I have "organized"—that word comes up again—two local care assistants to come in on a rotating basis.

Nira: Brian, what would be the ideal thing to do?

Brian: My own definition of the ideal thing to do is probably the one that I shall arrive at in the end. The ideal thing would be for me to move home and look after him. The difficulty for me is dealing with guilt from not doing this.

Nira: At the moment, we are dealing with the alternatives, one of which is seeking all the community help which you are currently in the process of organizing. You have said that you have never trusted your father to be able to cope adequately. He is now facing an objectively severe situation. Despite the help provided, he will be coping by himself. Brian is obviously concerned because, if his father can't cope in a normal situation, how is he going to cope now? The ideal situation would be, as Brian pointed out, to move home. Even if he did this for only the next 6 months, and if "home" was used only as a place to sleep. This would then mean that Brian was in control of the situation. It would clearly be the best thing to do. How difficult would it be in practice?

Brian: It would be almost inconceivable for me to do this. In practical terms, I would find it difficult but not impossible. Emotionally, I would find it extremely hard.

Nira: I think that all of us here will understand very well the problems of moving into such a situation. Could you explain to us why you find it so inconceivable?

Brian: It took a very long time for me to leave my parents and establish my own life. The process took several years beyond when I left home at 16. Now, although I can go home at Christmas and stay for a couple of nights, it's a problem for me to stay there for a longer period. I find myself becoming irritable, short-tempered, and frustrated, and feel an urgent need to get out of the situation. If I were to go home now, I would perceive this as an immense step backward.

Nira: Brian, could I suggest that perhaps you are operating under a certain assumption? Is it possible that you could look at this as a project? Whether you live with them or not, you are actually becoming their parent. I have several reasons for proposing taking care of your parents as a project. First, it offers an immediate means of coping with the situation. If you make that decision and abide by it for the next 3 months, then within that period, both your father and your mother will be back home. Then you will have another 6 weeks with them to help them accommodate to their new life. If you decide to move in with them for 3 months, you will bring new order into the household. They will have to adjust, and you will be able to take charge without opposition.

Second, you will have the opportunity to better understand yourself and why you have to keep such a tight grip on your independence. Why is it still shaky? And why are you still in danger of regression if you stay any longer than a week? Why is it still so irritating and difficult for you? It could be that this difficulty is not limited to dealings with your parents only. You mentioned your partner in business, and, of course, there may be other areas which we haven't touched on. In crisis work, we are confronted with an identified problem, but often this is not the real or the whole issue. It comes through very clearly that you are not going to neglect your parents and, therefore, it raises the question why your independence appears so shaky. I think that perhaps this is something for you to look into. Does this make any sense to you?

Brian: Oh, dear.

Nira: Could you imagine two small boys playing table tennis on the beach? If you watch their faces, you will observe an interesting phenomenon. On one boy's face, you will see an expression as if he is only responding to the attack of the other player. The other boy will give the impression that he is setting up all the shots, as if he were calling the tune. Yet a game of table tennis is a 50-50 proposition.

Half the time the ball is on one side of the net, and half
the time it is on the other. It is very much the same when
you are dealing with people, some of whom feel that they
go through life merely responding to situations. Many times
they don't realize that they too can throw the ball and not
just respond to it.

What we are discussing here is the question of control.
When a person has good control over life, he learns to face
new situations easily. He learns the rules and controls the
situation. However, as soon as he starts to defend his control, he becomes constrained and can only function within
very limited boundaries. I sense, Brian, that although you
are very much in control, you are also anxious. Going home
to your parents isn't actually "going back." It is, in fact,
an entirely new situation. The rules adopted by both you
and your parents will also be different.

Brian: Apart from the emotional feelings that I have about
going home, there is also the day-to-day matter about the
amount of time I need to devote to my job. My business, a
gymnasium and a health club with about 1,200 members,
is up and running 7 days a week. It is very involving and
I work 70 hours a week. I work alongside my partner, and
we have four staff members working for us. I love what I
am doing. We also have a small, up-and-coming property
venture, which consumes a great deal of my time. What I
do is much more demanding than a full-time job. At the
moment, it has become very much a way of life. My parents
live almost an hour's drive from the business, and since
we don't normally close up until the late evening, it would
be difficult in practical terms for me to move home.

Nira: Yes, it would be difficult, but not impossible. If you made
a few changes in your life, it might also not be that difficult.
Once you have settled this in your own mind, all the rest
will come easy. At this point in time, and this is very much
part of being in a crisis, you can only see the next day or
next week. Your parents are relatively young, and you
may find it necessary to make accommodations for many
years. What has taken place has undoubtedly been a shock
for you. In reality, it is just the beginning since your par-

ents will be needing care for a very long time. For your father, one of the main things he can enjoy is the feeling of security, knowing that he is being cared for. If you decided that you were going to give it a good shot (and this would mean you being there), then it is possible that it wouldn't be so bad. Is this something that you feel you could consider?

Brian: I don't find the long-term problem as difficult to deal with as the short-term problem. The house that they live in is actually much larger than they need. It is also expensive to run. It has been agreed among the family that the house will be sold and that they will buy a bungalow.

Nira: Where?

Brian: There is actually some debate about this. My sister wants them to move nearer to her. This would put them about 100 miles away from London. I think that it would be a great mistake. My brother-in-law is 22, just beginning his profession and likely to change jobs in the foreseeable future. If they left Northampton, my parents would then be left alone, more than 100 miles from anyone they knew. They have lived in their present location for more than 30 years and have built a life for themselves. My mother is also very involved in the community. I keep going on about guilt and you keep stopping me from expressing it.

Nira: You can express it as much as you like. All I was seeking to do was to clarify the distinction between guilt and guilt feelings. Martin Buber,* in his article "Guilt and Guilt Feelings," reminds us that we have been swayed by the notion of guilt feelings to the point where we forget that guilt still exists, both simple guilt and existential guilt.

Dealing with one's parents, especially in old age and deteriorating circumstances, brings out the real guilt of not doing enough for them, not doing what we would have done for our own children in the same situation, or what our parents did for us.

Brian: Do you know I actually resent them for doing this to

*Buber, M. (1963). Guilt and guilt feelings. In M. Freedman (Ed. and Trans.), *Pointing the way: Collected essays.* New York: Harper & Row.

me? That is an illogical feeling. Life is so organized and going so well. I am having a great time, and I've got independence. Now they go and do this.

Nira: Would you mind if I opened this up to the group? How many of you have experienced similar feelings?

[Many in the group raise their hands.]

Brian: I know that it is illogical.

Nira: It is not illogical; it is actually happening. It's a part of life, and you are angry with them because it is a tragedy for them and you.

Brian: It was odd going to see my mother the first time that she had a heart attack. It was very hard for me to see her hooked up to machines and looking so old, so small, and so helpless. It was less difficult for me to cope with seeing my father, even though he was in a much worse state and will probably never regain full mobility.

Nira: When you go through such a process with old people, you reflect yourself in them. It's like a vision of what may happen to you.

Brian: Death frightens me enormously. I don't think that it frightens my parents very much. For me, it is very difficult to deal with.

Nira: Is it death, or old age and the accompanying limitations?

Brian: I always say that you are as old as you feel.

Nira: Has being young and healthy been important to you all your life? Have you ever changed your values? Was there ever a period in your life when you thought that other things were more important?

Brian: It comes low on my list of priorities because it has always been there. Even though I smoke and am overweight, I have never been ill or broken any limbs. Security is my main priority, and the bottom line is maintaining the ability to make my own decisions and determine my own life.

Nira: This seems almost paradoxical. As social beings, none of us actually lives alone without connecting to others. Can we truly have our own life? To some extent, you do have your own life, but you also care for your parents. Someone who truly has his own life doesn't love anyone. Who wants to have this sort of life?

Brian: I accept that I am immensely selfish. Working for myself, I do what I want, when I want.

Nira: Could you tell us how selfish you actually are?

Brian: I like it my way.

Nira: That's close, but that's not selfish. [Laughter.]

Brian: If I want to do something, I don't like others standing in my way. If I want to go out, then I do so.

Nira: You sound like a teenager.

Brian: There is a lot of teenager in me.

Nira: What about this selfishness? How does it fit in with your work with old people and your involvement with social work?

Brian: I enjoyed what I was doing and was very good at what I did.

Nira: So where is the selfishness?

Brian: In my not wishing to be accountable.

Nira: In what way can this be viewed as being selfish? You still seem to feel the need to clearly state your desire to do your own thing, even though you have probably been doing it since the day you were born. It seems as if you are surrounded by ghosts who continually remind you to say, "I'm going to do my own thing."

Brian: These ghosts were probably the result of spending 8 years at a very repressive boarding school.

Nira: Were you physically abused?

Brian: No.

Nira: Were you the subject of ridicule at school?

Brian: My adopted role at school was that of the buffoon. I loathed school and was expelled from my first school for simply being too difficult.

Nira: Many of those here are familiar with the psychologist Alfred Adler, who gave us the idea of inferiority feelings and their compensation and overcompensation. You have had this difficulty with discipline in school and in childhood. Guess what this person chooses to do for a living? He runs a gymnasium. And what is a gymnasium all about?

Group: Discipline.

Nira: Yes. Organization and discipline.

Brian: I would say that institutions can be horrible, but also extremely easy to live in.

Nira: Providing, of course, that you are running them! [Laughter.] It would appear that there is a strong identification with law and order in your life. It could also be that you have an idealistic approach regarding how institutions should be run.

Brian: Yes.

Nira: A person who is as organized as yourself must act within a certain frame. Your gymnasium must also be quite an organization, with strict rules to allow it to function. You talk about needing to be free to do your own thing, and yet you work 70 hours a week. You are part of an institution which, although it is run by you, also controls you. The image of freedom that is so important to you has nothing to do with your life today. We form a self-image at a very early time in life. It is something that is very difficult to break. We may change the content of our life, but we keep the image. You certainly have a clear image about institutions. Does it include the family institution?

Brian: I just don't wish to have children. I assume that there is something automatically wrong in this. There is nothing about me that says that I want my family to go on when I am dead.

Nira: But why after you have gone? You would have a family to belong to and enjoy. You keep coming back to the word *selfish.* Could this be mistrust within yourself? There seems to be a division in your life between things that are clearly defined, such as running the gymnasium, in contrast to the emotional parts of your life where the rules are not so clear.

Brian: I have an odd relationship with rules, discipline, and organizations. I don't think that I have a need for rules, and I am not what I would consider rigid. I also don't conduct my relationships and friendships along specific guidelines. Very often my social interactions are played according to other people's rules. Discipline, however, is an issue that I have found disturbing. For example, I have tried many times, without success, to give up smoking. Each time, I seem to be reinforcing my own failure.

Nira: Let us return to the question of guilt. Could you consider focusing on the next 2 months with your parents? Would it be possible for you to consider moving in and taking over the organization? This, of course, would mean making adjustments at the gymnasium, arriving later and leaving earlier. Would it be possible for you to consider this? And please remember, it is not regression.

Brian: My immediate reaction is to say that there is no way that I would ever be able to go back and move in with them. Not at this present moment in time, or even in the immediate future. I may be able to consider it intellectually, but I don't know that I would ever be able to do it.

Nira: I am only asking you to consider it. You know how important resourcefulness is in life. Many people are not resourceful at all, living on what I term as *automatic pilot.* It sounds like your responses are decided by an automatic pilot, as if you know what to expect in any given situation. Brian, you now find yourself in a new situation, and I am suggesting that you be resourceful and not reject any solution out of hand. I realize that you are currently under stress, but if you are willing to consider new solutions, anything is possible. And bear in mind that this is not "going back." After all, it wasn't yesterday that you left. I am asking that on this occasion you don't allow the automatic pilot to make the decision for you.

Brian: Actually, it is very difficult to turn off the automatic pilot.

Nira: That is why most of your life is so routine. Some people are in even more danger because their automatic pilot functions so very well. The better it functions, the more routine and banal life becomes. It is a trap and I think that maybe you have fallen into it because you are anxious not to disturb the harmony that you have built for yourself. Try if you can to be task-oriented and not self-oriented because it seems that you are the only person who can cope with your parents' new situation. It is not important whether you decide to move home or not, but it is important that you consider it. Let go of the automatic pilot.

Brian: It would be very easy to say yes, and the truth is that I will try. The solution that I will probably end up adopting is the one that involves the least self-sacrifice.

Nira: I don't believe you.

Brian: The biggest self-sacrifice for me would be to go home and the least self-sacrifice would be for me to hire other people to do what I should be doing.

Nira: Whatever you decide will be difficult. None of it is easy. In a situation such as this, there are no good solutions. However, you *will* survive. Further, you sound the least convincing when you speak of making no sacrifices.

Brian: I really don't know that there is such a thing as altruism in anyone anymore.

Nira: Have you ever heard people say, "If I were in a dangerous situation, I would not choose to depend on this guy?" Brian, I would choose you in such a situation. I trust you.

Brian: I feel that I want to thank you for this evening, but I find it very difficult to say. I would interpret what you have just said as a compliment. We have talked a lot about rules and organization. In the end, a crisis like this is all-consuming for me. The anger that I felt last night was an all-consuming anger. I am not used to being undisciplined. It is like being on a roller coaster, very painful and very disconcerting. I rush back to work for stability. Sitting here, I have been quite calm and collected. I wanted to convey how I actually felt about the situation that I am in.

FEEDBACK

Group: Listening to this session tonight, I felt that you tried to repackage a solution that you felt was appropriate for him to take. I am not sure whether he accepted it.

Nira: In a way, Brian is in an impossible situation. If he didn't have this kind of attitude and responsibility, his predicament would not be that difficult. I suggested to him that the thing he knows should be done is the one thing he does not want to do. I asked him to consider it as an alternative and I'm sure that he will. My guess, however, would be that he will not go back. I suggested that it would be good for a while for him to return home and run things. Going through the process of making a decision about this matter (even if he doesn't return home) will serve three purposes. First, by considering this solution, he will not be in chaos for the moment. I also suggested that he switch to a new role between himself and his parents. I think that this could be very therapeutic for him. I think you could all see how afraid Brian is of intimacy and emotional ties. Finally, we can draw distinction between guilt and guilt feelings. When someone repeats, "I'm selfish, I'm selfish," what I actually hear is "I'm good, I'm good."

Brian is not a person who doesn't care. The purpose of this evening, was to help him out of his immediate crisis, his not knowing what to do. Brian struck me as someone who is completely trustworthy, someone who cares for people and will find solutions under stress. From this evening's proceedings, we can see a clear distinction between crisis intervention and therapy. Tonight we dealt with a given situation—information about his background was only relevant to the degree that he has got in touch with it.

Group: I don't think that he has come out of crisis because as yet I don't really think he has got in touch with it.

Nira: On the other hand, there are different phases of crisis. Tonight, he came out of chaos and, for someone with a great need to control, this is perhaps the worst stage of all. He has had a chance to reappraise his situation and the possible alternatives. More importantly, he has had an opportunity to face some of his own feelings. As far as his own problems are concerned, I think that we barely touched on them. His crisis occurred because he suddenly became very helpless. I have no doubt that, going away tonight, he will at least consider what was said.

POSSIBLE GAINS OF THE SESSION

Brian will find the best solution possible. Our task in this one-time intervention was to clarify, to open up options—even the one the person fears most of all. It was also to help the person go back to common sense and, most of all, to reflect to him that he is able to find his way out of the maze.

5

Joanne: Separation Crisis

INTRODUCTION

Joanne was undergoing a long period of stress. This prolonged situation was very alarming to her and periodically created crisis. Stress triggered by separation occurs often in relationships, and, in this session, we were primarily concerned with fostering an immediate behavior change and helping her regain control. We used an exercise aimed at regaining strength—here and now.

SESSION DIALOGUE

[As she enters the room, the group stares at Joanne. She is a very attractive woman, dressed in a provocative way, and looks very young.]

Therapist: Joanne was sent to me by her therapist, who was
   unable to help her in any of the problems that she presented. She came with very bad palpitations, what her
   therapist called panic attacks. She felt that since she was
   a child, life had been a terrible drag and that she was only
   alive now because of her two children. She is an attractive
   woman, with the persona of a bright, intelligent, and ar-
   ticulate individual. She has just celebrated her 40th birthday—a landmark in her life. She married at 29, not for
   love, but for children and companionship. There was no
   pain in her life, and now her crisis is both genuine and
   deep. Her father is a successful artist and she adores him.
   She says she is supposed to be the "up" character, but in
   reality, she doesn't want this. The crisis itself actually
   occurred last September with the end of her relationship
   with a man whom she had been living with for almost 2
   years. This man left her having said that he would marry
   her. Now Joanne is alone, something that she really hates.
   Over the past few months, she has lost considerable weight
   and her panic attacks have become particularly severe.

   [The therapist has introduced Joanne as if she is not
   present. She takes the lead from there and goes on to in-
   troduce herself. Joanne actually appears not to want to be
   interviewed. Without waiting for Nira to begin, Joanne
   starts the session.]

Joanne: Last Friday, I went to my therapist and told her that
   I felt hopeless and that I was in as bad a state as I was
   when I first came to her.

Nira: Was this the first time in your life that you ever went
   for help?

Joanne: No, in my late teens I went for help and had therapy
   to get me over a bad patch.

Nira: This was a very long time ago. What has happened now?
   What is your crisis all about?

Joanne: It appears on the surface to be very boring and mun-
   dane. The man I've been living with for 2 years left me—
   that's all. It's a simple thing which one would expect to
   get over relatively easily. For some obscure reason, I didn't
   and just broke down. I am normally in control of my mind

and my body. What is so terrible is that now I have ceased to be in control of any part of me. My body has gone to bits.

Nira: What do you mean by that?

Joanne: Anything can trigger off these panic attacks. They can last for up to 5 hours and my heart rate goes up to 140.

Nira: When did you have the last attack?

Joanne: Yesterday.

Nira: Could you describe it? When did it start? How did it happen? And when did it end?

Joanne: My ex-boyfriend's new girl bought a flat in the street next to mine. She's moved into the very street where I do my shopping and where my children go to school. When you break up with someone, the best thing to do is get rid of all those signs that remind you of him. It's very hard when she's living practically next door. I thought there was no risk of seeing her when I went to the post office yesterday. But when I saw her, bang! It hit like a burst of adrenalin. I felt sick and nauseous, and my heart started racing. I couldn't get out of the street fast enough, and when I got home I wept and howled and was a completely different person.

Nira: How long did this attack last?

Joanne: Not long, I have beta blockers from my doctor, and when I took one, my heart rate went down within 45 minutes. Before I had these tablets, I was out of control. It was like being drunk. I tried all sorts of things—relaxation, yoga, etc., but they don't really work if you are tense.

Nira: So when you took the pill, it helped?

Joanne: Yes, but I was shaking and nauseous for the rest of the day. I normally try to put up a good front, but on this occasion, I just went to bed and hid, and in the evening I was totally withdrawn. I had a friend over for supper, but I was so distraught I couldn't even hear what she was saying.

Nira: If you were in a position to change one thing, what would be the first thing that you would change to get out of this crisis situation?

Joanne: My jealousy. Because I truly believe that without that I could really function.

Nira: Is jealousy a new phenomenon in your life?

Joanne: Yes, I never felt jealous before.

Nira [to the group]: Let us look for a moment a little more deeply into this question of jealousy. It is generally believed that jealousy involves another person, someone who possesses something that we want. But it can also involve the extreme anguish that comes from being without something that is terribly important. What we must be clear about, however, is the difference between real and imaginary jealousy because every jealousy has a real and an imaginary element to it. In *Othello,* his jealousy was certainly very real from an emotional sense, but it bore no relation to reality.

At this point, it would be beneficial to consider the characteristics of jealousy and related emotions such as tremendous anger, hate, craving, and pain. Included in this list might be a sense of failure, but care must be exercised not to equate losing out to someone else in a situation such as this with failure.

Joanne: On one level, failure doesn't enter into it, but in another way, there is a terrible feeling of failure, that I could have done something to prevent the situation.

Nira: But what?

Joanne: I know that his involvement with this girl is just a passing whim and I realize that it is pathetic. I know that he and I are much better suited to each other and that, with any luck, she will go away. I am jealous of this girl because she now has his company, which I used to enjoy, and I am left with nothing except my children and a boring job. She has his body, his jokes—everything, and I have nothing. It's greed as well as jealousy. It's total emptiness; it's very childish.

Nira: How long is this going to last?

Joanne: I don't know.

Nira: Could you make a guess? Will your jealousy be acute for the whole year? [To the group:] The role of guessing and imagining is an important facilitator in healing. We always have a plan or guess about how things will proceed for us, and we follow it. When confusion sets in, we have lost touch with our plan. Thus we may complain of jealousy, but we really don't want to let go of it because giving up the pain is also giving up the person. The only thing that still "connects" Joanne to her ex-boyfriend is the jealousy. To give up the jealousy and the person is a very aware decision to make.

Joanne: I can no longer make any decisions; this jealousy has taken me totally by surprise.

Nira: We are guessing now, not making decisions. How long do you think that it will take?

Joanne: Until they get out of my life, and I don't have to see them on my doorstep.

Nira: Is that possible?

Joanne: Yes, I am considering moving to another house because I don't think that I can cope with it.

Nira: So this is one possibility. If not, how long will it take?

Joanne: If he were to split up with her?

Nira: But that is something over which you have no control.

Joanne: Then until something fills the void in my life.

Nira: Don't rush. We are speaking now of possibilities and are trying to make guesses. You are not in a unique position because I am sure many people have felt jealousy sometime in their lives.

Joanne: As you have described, I am sure that in essence jealousy is anger and holding on. However, I am not sure that giving it another name would necessarily transform the emotion.

Nira: We are not trying to transform your emotion, because jealousy is a feeling that takes at least a couple of months to dissipate. It might, however, be useful to call it helplessness, if this is what it is.

[To the group:] Joanne has no way of regaining the man whom she has lost. She is helpless. However, she may change this helpless situation by becoming powerful or potent in another field. It won't solve the problem with this man, but it may alleviate the terrible feeling of impotence and helplessness. When you tell an individual to do this, he or she will invariably ask how it will help with the problem. However, this takes trust and collaboration. I do not know whether Joanne trusts her therapist enough.

Joanne, I don't think we can really help you on the jealousy part. You'll get over it because people do. Once you decide to give him up, the jealousy will be healed. In a way, jealousy and anger replace the pain of separation. But I think we can help you with the symptoms of what you are actually undergoing now, namely the anxiety attacks. Are you eager to get rid of them?

Joanne: Yes.

Nira: When these attacks take place, you take a pill and they do go away. Why is this not a satisfactory solution for you?

Joanne: It's an easy solution. I don't know whether it's a good solution; that would depend on how you look at life.

Nira: How do you look at life?

Joanne: There are times when you have to cope, so you take an aspirin for headache. If there are times when I know that I have to cope, then I take a pill. (My children have suffered a lot.) Taking a pill has been what has kept me going.

Nira: So, the medication for these anxiety attacks is working.

Joanne: I take very little, I wait until the last moment because I know that it isn't an answer.

Nira: This may sound provocative, but why isn't medication a good solution for the time being? Anxiety is a very bad thing; what is worse than this? Taking a pill?

Joanne: No, the sense of failure for not handling it by myself. I feel a terrible sense of failure. I must do it myself. That's why I don't like taking pills—I'm not going to get hooked on them. I don't like taking pills because I'm a fighter, and I'm fighting all the time—I'm fighting to do it on my own . . . but failing.

Nira: Then, to fight it on your own with no medication would be a better solution for you?

Joanne: Absolutely.

Nira: So when you get palpitations and anxiety attacks, how could you fight it? What would be your techniques to help yourself?

Joanne: None of them work.

Nira: What have you tried?

Joanne: Breathing exercises, hot baths, watching television, and running.

Nira: I would like to make a point to you, but in order to do so, I would like you to do an exercise here on the floor. Would you agree to this?

Joanne: All right.

Nira: I want you to lie on the floor and five people from the group will hold you down. What I want you to do is break free. Use whatever method you choose.

[Joanne gets down on the carpeted floor. Five volunteers get up, although somewhat reluctantly. Their task is to hold Joanne down, to keep her pinned to the floor, not to let her break free. Joanne is a slightly built woman, which makes the group uneasy. To them the exercise seems patently unfair and stacked against her. The five strategically pin her shoulders, arms, and legs to the floor and hold her as tightly as they can. Much to their surprise, she kicks them off and breaks free in about a minute. She hits and bites and kicks, absolutely determined to break loose. The surprise in the room is total. The five amazed volunteers are left lying scattered on the floor. Joanne breathes deeply and gets up. The group is stunned by the unexpected result. Quiet falls over the room, and then the group begins to reassemble and resume the session.]

Nira: How did that feel?

Joanne: I feel free, I feel as if I have achieved something.

Nira: Does it make a connection for you?

Joanne: You would think it would be very difficult to break free of five people who were holding you down so tightly. In fact it was simple. I wouldn't have believed it if I hadn't done it.

Nira: I also think that it took only a very small effort on your part to succeed in breaking free. Did this exercise make any other connections for you?

Joanne: Because I feel physically very hemmed in, I find that exercise has a particularly beneficial effect. Right now, I feel powerful, in control. My heart beats regularly despite

the effort. I don't believe it. There was no anxiety. That is
how it connects—no anxiety.

Nira: What is the worst part about having an anxiety attack?

Joanne: Being out of control.

Nira: Are you really out of control? You may have palpitations
of the heart, but this doesn't mean that you are out of
control. If you don't take any action, how long do these
attacks normally last?

Joanne: Five to 6 hours.

Nira: You know that you can survive this time.

Joanne: But it makes dealing with anything completely impossible. I have to cope with my family.

Nira: All the time?

Joanne: Yes, absolutely.

Nira: In what way? Are your children never at school? What
happens when you suffer a panic attack at work.

Joanne: I carry on working—at least I appear to do so.

Nira: So it is possible. You can live through an attack.

Joanne: Yes, I'll survive.

Nira: How many attacks have you had in the past 2 weeks?

Joanne: They used to come every day, but now they come less
and less. In the past 2 weeks, I have had four or five.
However, I have been ill and, strangely, that seemed to
take over. On the whole, the triggers for the attacks were
diminished.

Nira: Why do you think that when you are really sick you
don't get anxiety attacks? It could be that when you are
sick you give up responsibility for yourself and you therefore don't need these panic attacks. It could also be that
these attacks are a way of hiding emotions. Having an
anxiety attack helps you not to cope. Does anything that
I have said strike a chord with you?

Joanne: No, because all through this affair I have been coping.
These attacks have only prevented me from coping really
well. Coping is just managing. These attacks have prevented me from being a proper mother for almost 5 months.

Nira: Referring to your last sentence, I would like to ask you
a difficult question. You say that you have not been a proper
mother for 5 months. Has it perhaps been longer than that?

Joanne: Until he left, I was a proper mother.

Nira: Could you describe the relationship that you have with your children?

Joanne: I have a 10-year-old daughter and a 7-year-old son. I have been a single parent for 5 years. Their father is around and very supportive. My son likes having men around, and when Mick moved in, he was very loving to the children, who, in turn, were very affectionate to him. However, when he came, I made sure that the routine I had built up wasn't disrupted. Since he left, I have gone to pieces. I haven't been a good mother because I haven't been responding directly to them. It is as if there is something between us.

Nira: Do you have any idea why Mick left?

Joanne: Yes, he left because he was screwed up. He was married for 15 years, and then his wife ran off with his best friend. He had never been on his own, and not having ever been independent was eating away at him.

   In retrospect it would have worked. But I've been very insecure, and I thought that once he had gone . . . . Anyway, I feel that all men have it easy.

Nira [to the group]: Moving quickly from one explanation to another, as Joanne has been doing here, is something that many of us tend to do. She wants to explain to us what happened and one way to do that is to generalize with statements like "all men" and "insecure." There is no logical progression to what she is saying; it is as if she doesn't really know what has happened and doesn't want to try to understand. As Joanne explained things, the routine went on very much as if he wasn't there. In a way he didn't matter, because the triangle was kept as before.

   [To Joanne:] Why was it important for you that he moved in?

Joanne: I fell in love with him. It wasn't a conscious decision. But within 2 days, he had stayed the night, and then he just didn't seem to leave.

Nira: But things happen that way in your life. If someone had asked you what you saw for the future, what would you have said?

Joanne: I wouldn't have said anything. People did ask what we were doing, but we were in love and therefore went ahead anyway.

Nira: Do you have a low frustration point? Do you like to have things you want without delay?

Joanne: Yes.

Nira: Could you give an example with relationships of not being able to delay satisfaction?

Joanne: Three years ago, there was a man and one evening we were sitting around. I was so tired that I couldn't be bothered to throw him out. I told him that if he wanted to come upstairs with me he could, and he did.

Nira: We are speaking about a low frustration level. Could you share an example that is more than just one minute or one evening? Can you recall a situation where you had the feeling "I must have it now, and in order to get it, I must bring myself to a certain state of emergency." If we observe a new baby, we see that when it is hungry, it cries as if it will die if food is not immediately provided. When it is 6 months old, it still cries but it hears its mother making noises in the kitchen and knows that food is coming. It is therefore able to relax. This is the start of abstract thinking—"I can't have it now, but I'll have it in 5 minutes." When the baby is 2 years old, it can accept having to wait until after dinner before having chocolate. At the age of 5, the child may want a bike, but can wait until Christmas or a birthday before receiving it.

When we can't tolerate the waiting, we put ourselves into a state of emergency: "If I can't have it now, I'll never have it." Later in life, we call this state frustration or delay, although for many adults, the feeling of delay is identified with "I'm never going to have it." The baby feels much the same when it is waiting to be fed. When we see an adult behaving in Joanne's own words "childishly," then we know that this person is headed toward a state of emergency. It is almost fatalistic: "If he doesn't come and live with me now, he will *never* come." Even though Mick might have left because he needed space and independence to cope on his own, Joanne only perceived it one way: "If I can't hold on to him totally, I don't have him at all." It's not even a question of not being able to delay. It's either now or never. This is why she loses her reality testing, and why, in truth, these situations become extreme and critical. As Joanne herself said, at home everything has to be perfect with the children. Life is seen as an ongoing task. As she said when talking about her children, "Yes I could cope, but not perfectly." She seems to doubt whether things will go right if she is not in control.

The word *control* comes up many times. We often forget that even when we don't *take* control, we are still in control, simply because we "are." We do not need special attention to be in control, only our brain and our senses. When we react in an extreme way, often it is because we don't believe that it will happen without special attention. Mick came in on an extreme impulse and, when he left, there was an extreme reaction. Does any of what I have been saying, make sense to you?

Joanne: It is 100% right.

Nira: Does it bring anything to mind from your past?

Joanne: I came from a strange family; my father is an *artist.* He himself lives a life of extremes, and nothing he says bears much relation to reality. He is a "larger than life" person, and I was brought up in a passionate, intense environment with everyone rushing around—an environment of eccentrics.

Nira: Are you eccentric?

Joanne: No.

Nira: Are you passionate?

Joanne: Yes, in everything that I do.

Nira: Passion and control have a hard time together—unless you can control your passion. [Laughter.]

Joanne: The man whom I work for says that I'm either incredibly happy or incredibly sad. I find it very difficult to occupy the middle rung.

Nira: So you're easy to predict because it is either/or for you.

Joanne: Yes, but you don't know which one. [Laughter.]

Nira: In a positive sense, what would you say is the opposite of a person who is predictable?

Joanne: Original.

Nira: In what way would you say that you are original?

Joanne: I make people laugh. [Laugher.]

Nira: Let us now turn to being authentic, to taking a calculated risk. Many people who appear to be spontaneous actually are not spontaneous, but possess the ability to process very quickly. To react in an extreme way is predictable, to do either/or is predictable. The truth about authenticity and predictability is that you cannot predict. Joanne, I would like to ask you again why Mick left?

Joanne: It was a combination of factors. There was the need for independence. But the final straw came when I over-reacted to some wasps, which had invaded the kitchen last autumn. For him, my making a drama out of this situation was the last straw.

Nira: How would life look without dramas?

Joanne: It would look pretty boring.

Nira: What drama are you in at the moment?

Joanne: It's just the extraordinary loneliness that is so hard. I don't see anybody now. I just drive to work, spend the day there, and come home to my two children. I don't go out with men on any level. It seems very hard, and I don't see any way out.

Nira: How long has this been going on?

Joanne: About 5 months.

Nira: What would your reaction be if I told you that in another 5 months it won't feel so bad?

Joanne: Say any date, and then I can knock the days off like a prison sentence.

Nira: Using your terminology, you are probably mid-term at the moment.

Joanne: If I could believe that to be true, I would be happy.

Nira: It is true, and it is also possible that the time span could be less. You could be further than halfway. Can you manage to survive this time without counting off the days?

Joanne: You might make me believe it.

Nira: I can't make you believe it, but I believe it. I used the figure of 5 months because you seem to be about halfway. For the next couple of months you won't see anyone and it is likely that you will continue to have anxiety attacks. However, as I see it, they could equally well stop overnight. They might return because for you they have become a habit. Why do I say this? When you meet a man who stutters and ask him how this started, he often gives an answer like "When I was 3 a dog jumped at me and made me so scared that I began to stutter." The point is not the effect of the dog, which may have lasted a couple of hours, but the impact of the stuttering, which served his personal goals and prompted him to continue stuttering into adulthood.

As far as the anxiety attacks are concerned, if you choose to undergo therapy, it should stop what you are experiencing at the present time. It will probably take a couple of months for the jealousy and sadness to dissipate. If you decide to take therapy, don't expect miracles. It would be good to learn to handle frustration, not because this is a particularly good thing, but because it is part of growing up. By so doing, you learn how to problem solve and to get along better with people. It is also possible to have natural highs without the need for dramas. I don't think you need your anxiety attacks anymore, and I stress again that I feel you are about mid-term in your current situation. I have a strong feeling that things will work out fine for you.

POSSIBLE GAINS OF THE SESSION

In summing up the session, the group and I identified three possible gains that Joanne could take away with her. The first is the negation of a connection between anxiety and madness. The second is the gain of experiencing her own power through the exercise and in reassuring all that she is already improving her state of being. The third, and not necessarily the last gain, is the time limit set for the duration of the crisis. As a consequence of that limit being set, she gained control over at least one element, namely time.

6

Jean and Harry: Parenthood in Crisis—Raising a Sick Child

INTRODUCTION

Jean and Harry present a unique example of people who survive for years with a chronic feeling of exhaustion and who are always on the verge of crisis. Their pediatric consultant, aware of their critical state, invited them to the workshop. They are the parents of two adopted children, 11 and 13, and have one of their own, who is sick. The intervention strategy attempted was to change their attitude toward their problems through new information about their child's educative difficulty, and to change their concept about their right to ask for help. In addition, we tried to offer an immediate option for relief, which was badly needed.

When the pediatrician introduced Jean and Harry, she told the group that she had known the family for a long time. She believed they were heading toward a crisis and that they needed to sort out their way of life before they were ready to treat their sick child. She spoke with warmth toward the couple.

The couple, both in their mid-40s, appeared to be very tired, expecting a lot from their work with us, and ready to cooperate. A few words of greeting were exchanged, and then the session got underway.

SESSION DIALOGUE

Nira: Could you describe the situation you are in now?

Jean: We had a child who wasn't planned. We hoped he would turn out to be whole and normal, but he turned out to be epileptic. He started out in a regular school but this didn't work out and he now goes to a school for the handicapped.

Nira: Why does he go to a school for handicapped children?

Jean: He can't cope with an ordinary school because he is unable to write properly. He also has a tremor and shakes.

Nira: Isn't that something that can be controlled by drugs?

Jean: No, He takes *epilin* and *mogodon* for his overactivity and also because he loses his concentration for long periods. This has meant that he has also had severe difficulty learning to read. However, he is using computers and word processors at school and this seems to be opening his mind. For much of the time, he is with children who are not running around. When we go to Sunday school or anywhere where there are children running about, he goes berserk. Because of this, we dread going out as a family.

During the last school term, we were all looking forward to going into town to do some shopping. Within 10 minutes of our arrival, Ben said his legs felt funny and I had to get us into the nearest shop. I had him on the floor and he started rolling around. This was not an actual epileptic fit but the feeling of other people watching and his brother becoming very frightened was most unpleasant.

Nira: How old is his brother?

Jean: His brother is 11 and he has an older sister of 13. Ben is 7. His sister copes with the epilepsy quite well, but it is normally when we go out that these things happen. I tried to get him into one of the changing rooms but I couldn't get him up on one of the stools. He kept rolling all over the floor. If you can imagine trying to hold on to this child while he is rolling on the floor. Well, it's just horrific. We've gone through it so many times, and I can't cope with it anymore. Something has to be done. The doctors are good to a point, but I feel we are going around in circles and getting nowhere.

Nira: Have you seen a consultant?

Jean: No. We are going to start doing that now.

Nira: Have you seen a neurologist? The reason I raise this question is that, from listening to you, I feel you have not yet learned much about his condition or the situation in which you find yourselves.

Jean: I am totally exhausted with it all. My husband and I have been married 23 years, and although we started courting when we were 15, I feel that, with all this going on, our marriage is slipping away. We are always so tired, and when you are tired, you don't cope.

Nira: Do you have a job away from the house?

Jean: I am a cashier at the school cafeteria for 2 hours every day, a job I started this year. I enjoy it very much because it is the only time I really feel in control of anything. When I get home it all caves in.

Nira: Harry, could you tell us about what you're doing, and how you are coping with this situation?

Harry: I'm a printer, which is a fairly demanding job. There are heavy production schedules throughout the day, and however much one kids oneself, one doesn't just switch it off in the evenings. I consider myself lucky in a way because Ben is a demanding boy who knows that he has problems. He is also at an age where he can understand and is frightened by his situation. He demands love, attention, and reassurance all the time. We try to the best of our ability to give him that reassurance. We've also got two other children. Coming here tonight Jean and I had the opportunity to talk to each other and we seem to lack enough of these sort of times. There is no chance in the morning because we are all rushing around, and I have to leave for work. Sometimes I really don't know how we cope. It is difficult for me because, being at work, I only see a small part of what is going on. But Jean has got it all the time. I expect she dreads it when Ben comes home at 4:00 in the afternoon. And that's a dreadful thing to say about someone who you love very much.

Jean: It makes you feel guilty, and I do feel very guilty. There are also times when I ask why was he born? Why did we have him? Even after all these years, sometimes I just don't want him. It makes you feel very guilty . . . and, in addition, we have your mother to deal with on Sundays.

Harry: On Sundays she spends the day with us.

Nira: Does she live alone?

Harry: Yes.

Nira: Are you the only child?

Harry: I have two sisters, but since she lives near us, we look after her.

Nira: Is this a recent arrangement?

Harry: Yes, since last autumn.

Nira: Has this added to the pressure on both of you?

Harry: Yes.

Nira: When she comes to the house, is she of any help? Does she give a hand with the children?

Harry: Basically she sits and chats and watches television. We also take her out for rides in the car. It's that sort of situation.

Nira: In what way does she disturb Jean?

Jean: She doesn't really disturb me. I just worry in case the children are upsetting her. It's just another hassle for me on a Sunday afternoon. I think that she needs her peace and quiet. So, in the end, I take the children out and leave her in the house. It's a way of solving the problem, because you can't let three children who want to run off some steam stay in the house in winter.

Harry: Yes, and something we have missed is that we live in an area where there is selective education. Our daughter is fairly bright, and for some mysterious reason, she has failed the 12+ examination. You probably think that this is a very common statement from parents whose child has just failed this particular exam. However, she really has been a very bright child all along. We then look at ourselves and wonder whether it is because of all the attention that we have given to our youngest. Perhaps it is this that has spoiled her chances. It is doubly concerning because our other boy is coming up to this exam as well. They are all very small bricks but when you put them together they become a rather big wall. What our therapist never mentioned was that we also fostered a child for 4 years and he was also a problem child.

Nira: When exactly was this?

Harry: It ended last year.

Nira: Why did you undertake a foster child given that you already had Ben?

Harry: At that stage, we could cope and didn't have any problems.

Nira: But why did you need another child? Was it a source of income?

Jean: No, we just wanted to give a child a home. We had three and felt we could cope with a teenager. For the first 4 years it was fine.

Harry: The financial rewards were very small. We just felt we wanted to do it.

Nira: A kind of contribution.

Harry: Yes. Toward the end he was a problem child. He couldn't stop himself from stealing. Eventually the court had to take him and put him in a special home. We obviously still follow his progress, but we don't have any direct involvement now.

Nira: What else?

Harry: Jean reached menopause very early—at age 45. You look back at where you are and what you are going to do. For myself, I have made the decision to change course as regards my job. I am quite happy where I am working but I feel I should be doing something else. In this regard, I am currently going through job interviews. I intend to stay in the printing field and therefore don't think that I will have a problem finding a job that I like.

Our major handicap at the moment is Ben. It is always difficult when you have a handicapped child because you

look at yourself and wonder whether you did anything
wrong. You wonder if you could have done something more
at the birth and tear yourself to pieces to see if you have
contributed in any way to the situation he is in.

Nira: Let me see if I understand what you have been describing
to us about your situation. Listening to you, there are
several things that come to mind. There are some general
things that occur with people in your situation and some
that are probably individual to you and the way you are.
Starting with the general things, one factor that comes
across clearly is that you are very responsible people. Responsibility is probably a high value for you both. You
possess a high degree of social interest and contribution.
You have adopted two children and have even fostered
another. Why would anyone voluntarily look for such trouble? Many parents find it difficult enough dealing with
their own children. The way you described it, it is as if you
thought that since you already have two school-age children, why not add a third? It sounds as if the decision was
just an everyday occurrence. It was not. Hard work, responsibility, and taking care of people are very important
to both of you. However, it would seem that in many in-
stances you have overdone it and spread yourselves too
thinly. I don't know whether it was Ben who was too much
or whether this is characteristic of your whole life together.

While you were talking, I found myself wanting to ask
whether either of you ever had any fun or a social life.
What do you enjoy doing? It seems that everything, including weekends and the shopping, is a task. Everything
you do is for the children and is done under pressure—
going shopping, coming back, preparing dinner, putting
the children to bed, getting everyone up in the morning
and then dashing off for the day. Often it is not what we
do that is significant but how we do it. It seems that for
you, life is enormous pressure. I don't underestimate the
difficulty you are having with Ben. I just want to check it
out with you. What has come through so far is that, in
addition to Ben, your whole life is pressure, one task or

responsibility on top of another. And this has been the case for many years. Have I understood you correctly?

Harry: Yes, very much so. The social side of our life has been reduced to perhaps one evening a week. Sometimes we may creep out on the weekend.

Nira: Do you have any friends?

Jean: Yes, and I like to cook.

Nira: So you enjoy cooking and invite people to dinner. But I am asking particularly about friends, not so much your social life or parties. Do you have any close friends, and do you see them often?

Jean: Yes. We get together once every 3 weeks or so.

Harry: With friends, you don't actually see them, rather you talk on the phone.

Jean: I've got a very close friend who I share things with.

Harry: And I have friends at work.

Nira: But life is still high pressure for you?

Jean: I would like so much to get off, but I can't.

Nira: Let's play an imaginary game. How would you choose to "get off" the pressure merry-go-round. Assume that anything is permitted, let your imagination go, go to the extreme.

Jean: I'd go into the sitting room and sit by myself in a chair with no radio, no noise, no anything.

Nira: But I'm offering you a better option—not just one evening but forever. What would you do? What would be your imaginary option?

Jean: The first thing I would do would be to make Ben well.

Nira: That is something over which you have no control. Could you attempt to rearrange your life within what is possible?

Jean: I don't think I could. I am trying to think how I could rearrange it.

Nira: There are two ways to look at any situation, one of which involves making practical changes. An example would be if you had a very bad marriage, you could move to get a divorce. However, you could also attempt to adapt better to the marriage. It is important to realize that there are always at least two options. You both live under excessive pressure, and this has a tendency to make people less rather than more productive. There is always more and more work to be done, yet you become less productive as the fatigue continues to accumulate.

As I mentioned, there are two options; one is to change the factual situation, the other is to change the attitude. If no practical change is feasible, a person can adopt a new attitude, even toward pressure and responsibility. At the present moment, you may feel that is impossible, and perhaps you are right. But what I am considering now are the changes, real changes, that can be made in your life, and even more crucially, the reasons for making them.

[To the group:] Jean and Harry have many purposes and goals in life. However, listening to them, it soon becomes clear that one issue that doesn't seem to be a goal for them at all is to live more fully, to enjoy life, and to do things just for themselves. They may have thought about it, but they have never practiced it. I also get the impression that doing this has never really been a goal for them.

[To Harry and Jean:] Am I right on this point?

Harry: Yes, I think you probably are. In fact, one of the things which we would suggest when our children grow up and have children themselves is that we would look after them on weekends.

Nira: I'm sure this would be the case, but, please, just for the weekend! So it would seem that you both have a perfect life. [Laughter.] What do you want to be different?

Jean: I want a bit more peace and quiet.

Nira: OK, but in general your life goes pretty much the way you have chosen, in that you devote yourselves to the children. You have adopted two children, and I'm sure you have made them very happy and given them a good and stable home. You are solid parents and warm people. You have also devoted 4 years to a foster child, perhaps the best 4 years of his life. So what is it that you both want? Let's get to everyday life and see what is possible.

Harry: For myself, I would like to spend more time with my wife—I think that this would be rather nice.

Nira: How could this project come about? Could you think of some imaginary plan, like going away for a week?

Jean: That would be lovely, but it would never happen because there is no one to look after the children.

Nira: Did you ever look for somebody to do this?

Jean: Yes, we have thought about this.

Nira: Yes, but did you ever look for somebody in a practical sense?

Jean: No.

Nira: Do you think that someone could replace you for a week, or are you irreplaceable?

Jean: Yes, of course someone could; it is just a question of finding the right one. My parents are out—we just couldn't leave until Ian and Carol are a bit older. We couldn't find someone for Ben.

Harry: We'd also feel very guilty if we arranged for someone to look after the children while *we* went away for a holiday or a break. It wouldn't be a break because we would feel guilty that we'd gone off and hadn't taken the children with us.

Nira: I think that guilt is a very strong issue for both of you. [To the group:] Anyone have a reaction to Harry's remark, "If we go away on vacation and leave the children, we wouldn't enjoy it because we would feel guilty"? Would any of you like to respond to this?

Group: It may well be a holiday for the children to be away from their parents for a while.

Nira: Could you imagine what it might do for these three children?

Group: See if your parents can come and stay and give you both a week's break.

Nira: But Harry and Jean don't want this break.

Group: The children might want them to have this break.

Nira: Don't use your best card like this. If we're going to manipulate them into having a vacation, let us do it slowly, so that they will be convinced by our argument. [Laughter.] Our only chance then is to convince them that it will be good for the children.

Pediatric Consultant: It seems to me that you have both been easy for your clever child to manipulate. It is quite apparent that you are very conscientious. Listening to your story about Ben when you went shopping made me wonder. If you saw a neurologist, you might find that Ben's behavior is not all connected with epilepsy. I am a doctor and have had experience dealing with epileptic children. Many of the children with whom I have contact use their epilepsy to ensure that everyone runs around after them. It might be useful to check it out with a neurologist. You may find that incidents like the one in the shopping center can be viewed on two levels. They can be traced to the effects of genuine epilepsy, but it might also be that Ben has discovered such incidents are good for getting attention. A break for you might lead to finding a different way of relating to Ben and to his epilepsy.

Nira: You are actually confirming what his own doctor said, namely that there are two different problems. There is no denial of the actual epilepsy. Even nonepileptic children take advantage of various situations in the same way to gain an excessive amount of their parents' attention. The late Dr. Rudolf Dreikurs* used to refer to such a situation as a "goldmine" for the child. It begins with a real problem, but the child quickly discovers ways to "mine the lode" to his or her own advantage because the child is miserable and sick and because this sickness frightens the adults. And it is rare when adults refuse the child's demands. Ben is getting a lot of attention without even knowing he is doing so. You are both easy to manipulate because you operate on guilt. It's as if you were put on this earth to do some penance, to make it up to him in some way, and you collaborate perfectly.

What we are suggesting is that your problem with Ben is an educational one. His sickness is one facet only, and I think you should seek professional help. Make an effort to find such help because Ben's misbehaving can be con-

---

*Dreikurs, R. (1984). *Multiple psychotherapy.* Chicago: Alfred Adler Institute.

trolled. I wonder if you haven't had the same kind of problems with the other children. You said that they are "only" 11 and 13. But other parents might just as easily say "Our children are grown up; they're 11 and 13." How much help do you get from the other children in handling Ben's handicap and problems?

Harry: Carol is superb and Ian blows hot and cold. Now that Ben is getting older, Ian has someone to play football with.

Nira: And yet neither of you believes you could leave for a couple of days with the children under supervision of an adult, even though you say the two siblings are "superb" with Ben. Although you are good at many things, you seem not very good at getting help.

Jean: It goes against the grain; I can't ask.

Nira: You *can't* ask. Of course there's more to it than merely asking. There is a myth about seeking and getting help. Giving help is easy because it is an ego trip; it is the giver who is significant, maybe even "holy." But when you seek help from someone else, you allow this individual to be significant. Many people seem so good because they help others all the time. But they never allow anyone to help them. Life does not have to be such an enormous pressure even when you have a handicapped child. To some extent, the epilepsy serves as a cover because you are not assertive enough in guiding him toward proper behavior. You feel guilty if you do something "wrong" to him, you feel guilty for bringing him into the world, you feel guilty for hating him some of the time. But it is OK. It is normal to ask why you had this child and why you couldn't have been satisfied with just the other two children. With handicapped or mentally retarded children, one of the biggest problems for the parents is the feeling of guilt for having brought them into this world.

I don't believe we are dealing with anything neurotic as far as the guilt is concerned. It's a natural and real feeling. But if you continue this way the situation will be difficult to correct and the attitudes and behavior will be ingrained for life. Ironically, the only way to learn not to feel so guilty is to give yourselves more of a life of your own. In a sophisticated and righteous way, you are driving yourselves to be victims. And that makes Ben's tyrannical hold over you seem monstrous at times. If you think about it, he is growing up among four adults, and there is no need for him to make life such a pressure for all of you. The more you become victims, the more monstrous he will become. The better you treat yourselves, the better Ben will be. Does this make any sense to you?

Harry: Yes. The disruptive behavior could well fall within the pattern you are describing. We interpreted this as his needing love and self-assurance. But in a family of five, you can't love one-to-one all the time.

Nira: You say that Ben needs self-assurance, but is what you are currently doing actually helping to build his confidence? I strongly suggest you attend a parenting group so you can learn how to cope better with Ben and learn to treat him as a normal person. Allow yourselves to ask and accept more help from others, from your children, your family, and even your mother. Could you imagine your mother coming on Sunday and leaving the children with her so you could go to the movies?

Jean: No.

Nira: What would happen? What do you believe you'd find on returning from the movies?

Harry: It would take both of us a number of days to recover. There would be some crisis. We would probably be called out of the cinema halfway through the movie.

Nira: I forgot to mention that you don't tell them what cinema you're going to. [Laughter.]

Harry: I'm not being flippant, but a crisis would be generated in some way.

Nira: Who would create the crisis?

Harry: Mother. And Jean's parents love having the children, but only one at a time.

Nira: If Jean's parents or your mother could listen to you at this time . . .

Jean: They'd be horrified.

Nira: Why? Don't they know anything about it?

Harry: No.

Nira [to the group]: You see what I mean. I speak now about not being able to ask for help. I think that even with a heart problem your mother would be able to stay with the children. There might be some chaos but why does this have to be a crisis? What could happen with the other children taking care of Ben? I don't think that either of you have had any experience asking for anything, not even from your parents. This could even include sharing with them how difficult your life is. What would be wrong with once in a while asking them to stay with the children so that you both could go away for the weekend?

Harry: If we asked our friends for help, I know that they would say yes and would be pleased to take the children for a weekend.

Nira: Have you ever done this?

Harry: But we don't take them up on it. We would never dream of asking our parents to do it. Probably because we are frightened that they might say no.

Nira: Maybe the relationship goes both ways. Since you have never actually asked them for anything, it is possible they don't feel meaningful at all. I don't know your parents but somehow I doubt that if you asked them that they would say no. You don't have to start out with a whole weekend. To begin, try just one day. I would like to suggest that you do something now. If your friends have indicated that they would be willing to help, take several days off and loosen up. Be together, discuss your job, and decide together how you are going to deal with the rest of your life. I think that *right now* it would be very good indeed if you could get away for a weekend. Ask your friends to take over all three children, because most of the help Ben needs, the older children would give. You may be really surprised how good the older two will feel about this, and Ben may surprise you too. Once you are both on your way, he'll behave much better. Why? Because other people will not deal with him in the same way as you do. Does this make any sense at all?

Jean: I think you get on a treadmill and it just goes on and on.

Nira: Like anything else in life, if you have a problem, learn about it and do something to improve the situation. I do hope you will be able to consider some of what has been said here tonight and that things will change for you.

POSSIBLE GAINS OF THE SESSION

The first likely gain from this session was the warmth and support Jean and Harry got from the group. At the end of the session, people spontaneously offered more suggestions, shared their own experiences, provided names of specialists, and invited them to visit. This support and empathy had a strong impact on the couple. Also the practical options that were offered suggested to them that the big problem could be cut into manageable pieces, which could be dealt with one at a time. The issue of asking for or receiving help is always crucial with people who *cannot* ask. By having the issue discussed at length in their presence, Jean and Harry may be encouraged in the future to accept and even ask for help from others. Finally, valuable information about getting the right treatment for Ben and suggestions about parent guidance groups may prove beneficial to them.

7

Debra: Cycles of Crisis

INTRODUCTION

Debra was different from any other counselee in this workshop because she was presented as a person in crisis, while, in fact, she was in a cycle well known to her and well controlled by her. Debra avoids crisis and survives in spite of self-induced provocations such as heavy drugs, a double life, and false reality testing. Because she was presented to us erroneously as a crisis "rape case," the session turned out to be more of a direct therapy session than crisis intervention. Consequently, we were more concerned with standing up to her challenge and not falling into her trap of high drama for its own sake and did not offer specific support. The main issue of the session was to help her look at facts in a different way and to trust her power of self-control.

The therapist introduced Debra by her first name, talked

energetically, apologizing for introducing a person to the workshop who went through a crisis some 5 years earlier. He gave the impression of being in an impasse himself in his therapy with her and described her present situation as a new crisis or maybe a repercussion of the previous one.

Debra was 35 years old, athletic, with long hair that covered half her face. With her big eyes she looked the group straight in the eye. Her full presence on the stage left the impression that she belonged there. She sat in a position from which she faced the group rather than me.

SESSION DIALOGUE

Therapist: I suggested that Debra come tonight because of her increasing difficulty in coping with life. She suffers a great deal of pain and anxiety, and has become dependent on the painkilling medication she has been taking for years. Her difficulties were exacerbated about 5 years ago when she was raped by a drug pusher. Debra is desperately afraid that her husband will find out about her double life. Although her problems date back quite some time, she is actually coming to a crisis point in her life now.

Nira [to Debra]: Could you give me a short description of what has been happening to you in recent weeks?

Debra: A few months ago, we began working on a production that had a great deal to do with rape and I began to feel rather disturbed. It has been some time since the rape incident happened, and I never really told anyone.

Nira: Did you tell your husband or go to the police?

Debra: No. Although in my professional career I had tackled a lot of comedy, when I undertook anything of a serious nature I just shut it off. In the past, I had a drug problem with cocaine.

Nira: How did this arise?

Debra: I have never been entirely certain. I was part of a generation that generally did things like that and when I went to the university, there was a great deal of cocaine readily available. Normally, I took it so that I could work harder.

Nira: What happened to you as a result of drugs?

Debra: I don't know.

Nira: So, if I have understood you correctly, it is since the start of this play that the rape incident has resurfaced on your mind. Would you say that the rape has had a lasting influence on you?

Debra: Yes, I do think that it has.

Nira: Could you tell us how this rape still influences you? Let me share some information with you. A rape is not a trauma from within but due to the direct intervention of someone outside. The appropriate response to such an event would depend on whether the individual gave a life-long significance to the event or whether, no matter how sad and traumatic the experience was, it was lived as an episode. It would also depend on the quality of support that the victim did or did not receive. This is why rape victims are encouraged to share and to talk about what they have undergone. Would you care to share with us a little about how it happened?

Debra: I think the whole experience must really have affected me, but then obviously it would. In the case of the rape, it seems I should have known that it was coming. Basically, my problems have been drug related. I don't always take drugs, but I regularly come back to them.

Nira: Did the rape happen with someone you knew?

Debra: Yes, it happened with the man who regularly supplied my drugs.

Nira: Although we are looking at a traumatic event that happened 5 years ago, I would like to suggest to Debra that it is not this event that is having such a long-lasting and profound influence on her life. Let me illustrate my point with an example of an individual who had a psychotic episode at the age of 20 and was hospitalized for 3 weeks. At the age of 40, he comes for marriage guidance counseling and the first thing he says is that he was hospitalized for 3 weeks. Only later does he acknowledge that this hap-

pened some 20 years ago. Now, 20 years later, he still
regards himself as someone who was psychiatrically hospitalized. Spending these 3 weeks in a mental hospital has
given him a self-image for life.

　　Five years ago, Debra was raped, not by an unknown
person when she walked in the street, but by someone she
knew. She also stated that at that time she was a lot more
dependent on drugs. My question to Debra as I listen to
her is why, after 5 years, this is still one of the first things
that emerges despite the fact that she continued to function
extremely well in other areas of her life. Does this make
any sense to you?

Debra: Are you saying that rape is not the central issue?

Nira: Yes. It is possible that you have begun to see it as the
central issue and have connected it with many other things.
Would it be helpful to you to share with us how it occurred
and why it has become such a central issue for you? Before
you answer, I would like to ask one other thing. You seem
a very open person, and yet you have kept the whole rape
episode to yourself. Did you feel ashamed or accused?

Debra: I didn't want anyone to know that I was taking a lot
of drugs.

Nira: In what way was it your fault?

Debra: I was living two separate lives, and I was taking drugs.

Nira: In what way did the incident have such an influence
over you, if it did?

Debra: After that, things came to a head. People found out
that I was taking drugs and I was forced to leave the area.

Nira: I am going to ask you a question that might appear to
be rather provocative, although I don't mean it in this way.
Since you were taking drugs, I would like to know whether
you suffered from hallucinations.

Debra: Not really.

Nira: Are you absolutely certain that you were raped?

Debra: That is an interesting question.

Nira: I am not concerned about whether you willingly slept
with this man, but whether the rape actually took place.

Debra: Well, yes.

Nira: Are you sure?

Debra: I think I am sure.

Nira: The reason I asked this question is that under the influence of drugs one becomes paranoid. As you yourself stated, you were living two lives and in constant fear of being found out. You were obviously under stress and feeling persecuted. In this situation, it is often difficult to tell imagination from reality. Do you have the rape clearly in your memory, or is it rather obscure? Did you have a relationship with this person?

Debra: I knew him, but I didn't have a close relationship with him.

Nira: Have you any idea why he raped you? Did he also take drugs?

Debra: He gave me drugs free of charge and suggested sexual favors in return.

Nira: What happened at this point?

Debra: It was when I refused to accept this arrangement that the rape occurred.

Nira: Did you cry for help?

Debra: I don't think so.

Nira: Would you say that you were in shock?

Debra: I was a bit in shock, but I laughed.

Nira: If we are looking back, shock is inappropriate behavior according to the situation. Would you say that you were in shock, or that you were in control of the situation?

Debra: I guess, looking back, you could say that I was in shock because I had to leave the show that I was in before the end of the run.

[Silence. Debra is left to reconsider the possibility of imagining the rape or cooperating under shock. She chose to switch back to the fact that she had to leave the show rather than think about the rape episode. After an extended silence, it is clear that we should open a new chapter. The silence was needed in order to proceed from the misleading introduction to reach for an understanding of the real issues that upset Debra's life.]

Nira: What has happened to you in the past couple of weeks?

Debra: I fear that I am going to start taking too many drugs and that the cycle will start over again.

Nira: How many times have you been through this cycle?

Debra: Many times.

Nira: Is it a cycle, or does it have anything to do with real life?

Debra: Aren't cycles part of real life?

Nira: Not necessarily. They are part of personality. Does your husband know about your situation?

Debra: He knows that I sometimes take too many drugs.

Nira: It would seem that he doesn't really know very much about the true situation. Are you afraid to share it with him?

Debra: Yes.

Nira: Do you think it might endanger the marriage?

Debra: To some extent; I'm really happy. What are we talking about? I'm starting to get really irritated. I did say that I would come this evening.

Nira: Debra, listen to me, there is no reason at all why you should get irritated. If you really don't know why you're here and would prefer to stop now, that would be perfectly OK.

Debra: I feel that I am taking an examination and not passing.

Nira: OK, let's stop now.

Debra: I don't mind talking.

Nira: The point is not whether we talk, but whether we can make a breakthrough in your present situation. I wouldn't use the word *help,* because you don't appear to be asking for help. However, it may be possible for you to view your current situation from a different perspective. Could I check with you, did anything that has been said here tonight make sense to you?

Debra: Everything has made a certain sense to me.

Nira: Could you give me an example of something specific?

Debra: That I might not be perceiving things as they really happen?

Nira: Do you have another example of mixing fantasy and reality from childhood and adolescence?

Debra: I used to have imaginary playmates, but I guess that is pretty normal.

Nira: Everything you are describing is pretty normal. Do you have a specific example of mixing fantasy and reality?

Debra: To a certain degree it all seems to be connected with drugs. I sometimes feel like a drug maniac. You know when you pretend things when you are a child and then they just become real.

Nira: With fantasy and reality, often it is not that we are unsure about whether an event is real, but that we are afraid to check and find out. If imaginary events occurred in everyday life, the natural inclination would be to ask and check. When you start to doubt yourself, it becomes difficult to remember what you have actually said and to whom. To a person in this situation, the main concern is being found out. What we are actually talking about is living in the enemy camp. Let me clarify what I mean by this. We all know about people who spend much of their lives spying in different countries. To survive these people have to obey three rules. The first rule is that if their friends and colleagues find out who they really are, then it is the end. The second rule logically follows the first. It is that in order not to be found out, they must not make any mistakes because mistakes could blow their cover and prove fatal. To allow them to survive under the stress of these two rules, the third rule states that all this is only temporary and that the real or "good" life will start at the conclusion of the current contract. It is as if the spy says, "I am not going to live all my life with this deception because one day this job will end and I can go home."

It seems to me, Debra, that what you are describing has a great deal to do with living in the enemy camp. Even in intimate relationships like the one with your husband, you are desperately trying not to be found out. In order to accomplish this, you endeavor not to make mistakes that will reveal you. However, this is strenuous because you cannot be on your guard all the time. When you begin to loosen up, it is very frightening for you. Does this make any sense?

Debra: Yes, you are freaking me out.

Nira: In what way?

Debra: It's like a really bad trip.

Nira: Does it make any sense?

Debra: Yes, it does.

Nira: Could you tell me in what way? What of these three things is most relevant to your life at the moment: not being found out, not making mistakes, or being on guard all the time?

Debra: I think all three.

Nira: If you could change one of these three, which would you choose to change? You see, it is possible for you to make the decision that this is life and not the enemy camp.

Debra: If I made the decision to change, would it then not be the enemy camp, even if it was still a concentration camp?

Nira: You create your own camp because you believe that if people know the truth about you, it will be fatal. However, you only believe this to be true. With your husband, you must be afraid that he would leave you if he knew the whole truth. If this were not the case, you would surely look to him for support by sharing. If you want to come out of the camp, he could even help you achieve this. I am also quite sure that your friends and colleagues know that you take drugs. One's use of drugs rarely remains a secret. In any event, what will happen if they do know about this? Will all your other qualities be forgotten? Will you be known only as someone who takes drugs?

Debra: It's very complicated. It's a question of keeping everything together and in check, and it is easier to act in check if you do some drugs.

Nira: In fact, many people do drugs for the opposite reason— to get rid of control. If I understand you correctly, you take drugs to be in even greater control, to keep a better check on life. What frightens you most of all? The limit?

Debra: It always starts out fine, and then I end up going past the limit.

Nira: Could it be that you experience control at the highest level? To keep under control under the influence of drugs is a terrific challenge. Most of us have a hard enough job keeping control of life as it is. You need to be in super control, and yet this is becoming more and more difficult.

[To the group:] The need to be in control is opposed to letting the natural flow of life take place. To flow does not mean to totally lack control or totally lose oneself. We are aware and conscious and decision makers at all times whether we acknowledge that fact or not.

The need for control means that we don't let ourselves flow the right way. It also means danger, and fear of being in touch with ourselves and maybe finding out that our "self" is rather an inner void, empty, nothing, boredom. The need for control and excitement all the time stems from the fear of touching the self—the void—death.

Debra: Actually, I am seldom bored.

Nira: Boredom is an existential phenomenon. What do you do not to be bored?

Debra: Sometimes when I take drugs, I can work harder and longer.

Nira: In what ways do drugs save you from boredom? Can you think of any theatrical figure whose life you have perceived as being very boring? In the play *Equus** there is a marked contrast between the boring life of the psychiatrist and the exciting life of the young and crazy boy. He envied the passion of the young boy. Debra, do we also speak about passion?

Debra: Yes, like acting, drugs seem to add a certain passion to my life, which on its own seems pretty disappointing. If it were possible to be high all the time and keep under control, that would be great.

Nira: I think here you are touching on a serious dilemma, wanting to keep high, but being unable to do so all the time.

Debra: I can't say that I am actually bored, just that I'm trying to make it less boring for all of you.

Nira: So it is one thing to be bored in life and another to be boring to other people.

Debra: It's fatal.

Nira: We were led in this session to deal with the issues of control versus the void. Now we touch on another vignette of boredom and that is not to be boring to others. Being ready to go to extremes can be predicted because enter-

*Shaffer, P. (1973). *Equus*. London: Deutsch.

tainment has to top itself all the time. When insignificance
is a person's impasse, he'll go to great length in all directions to become significant. That can include anything from
efficiency to sacrifice, knowledge, service, entertainment,
self-abuse, drugs, drama. The paradox of this situation is
that while you try to pretend that you are interesting, you
forget that in reality you *are* interesting.

Excitement is a problem because usually when we become dependent on excitement we rely on doing things in
one way. One of the purposes of therapy is to enlarge this
and discover safer ways of gaining excitement in life. On
the whole, Debra, you are in good control of your life. You
get close to a certain point, and then you retreat. I have
two pieces of advice, which you may care to think over.
First, check and recheck on questions of reality and fantasy
because you're losing touch when you don't know. Imagination is fine as long as it is not linked with reality. The
second point I would like to make concerns excitement,
because although you are in an exciting profession, it doesn't
seem to be enough for you. Perhaps it would be possible
to consider exploring another area of life that could be
stimulating in an intellectual way. At the moment, the
majority of your encounters are experimental—in drama,
in acting, and with drugs.

Debra: Nothing is entirely satisfying, but then this is the
nature of life in general.

[Silence. After Debra's declaration about life in general
being unsatisfactory, the session came very close to "boredom." The silence was broken by a sudden turn.]

Debra: I feel incredibly hostile, and I can't stand feeling hostile.
I can't believe this conversation, whatever it is.

Nira [to the group, half ignoring the challenge and coming
back to the issue of drugs and excitement]: It may seem
odd that a person would create concrete secrets about things
like rape, drugs, and crime when all along covering up
what he or she believes is the real secret, "I am worthless,
I am empty, I am nothing." The paradox lies in the fact
that the identified problem is much more dramatic and

dangerous than what the person perceives as the real problem.

Years ago, a girl of 7 said to me, "Today in my ballet class I watched the girl who is number one in our class, and I saw that she doesn't really know how to dance. She only pretends that she does." I asked her a difficult question: What is the difference between the two? Tonight we observe a person who believes she is not interesting and who only pretends to be.

Once you begin experimenting with drugs, being high becomes a very special kind of experience. Once you have decided that you want to replace it, the question is with what. How can you hope to break the cycle? Could you explore something else in your life, something to replace this, something you haven't yet tried?

Debra: I get highs from a lot of different things.

Nira: Do you give other people highs?

Debra: I think I do in acting and with my friends. I think people enjoy my company.

Nira: So it's not just getting highs, but giving them as well.

Debra: Making someone else happy. That's even better.

Nira: Would you say that high is happy, or is it perhaps more than that?

Debra: You can get highs and happiness without drugs, that's obvious.

Nira: I hope there is something from tonight that you may be able to take away and consider.

Debra: Actually, I feel much worse now than when I started.

Nira: I suggest that now would be a good point to end the session. For the next couple of days, try with the aid of a therapist to discover what has made you feel much worse. At the beginning of the evening, you seemed to take the proceedings very lightly, and then all of a sudden you began to feel hostile and worse. If you wish, it will be possible for you to come back for another short session before the end of this course.

Debra: Am I supposed to be honest? I feel very alien and I don't feel any warmth. Things were discussed very quickly, and then spot judgments were made. It seems like bullshit to me.

Nira: If it is bullshit, why should it make you feel worse? If it isn't, then I hope you will be able to take away just one idea from tonight to consider. Let me mention a few: living in the enemy camp, making a decision to move out of this camp, reality and imagination, and excitement. I am sorry that you feel worse, but I can't say that the time has been wasted.

[Debra leaves the room.]

FEEDBACK

Nira: I think the turning point for Debra tonight was being found out. For someone like Debra, being found out is the worst thing imaginable. She is probably extremely capable, but she is pushing herself to the point of no return. It is necessary for her to control her life under progressively more severe conditions, and this is rapidly becoming an impossible task. There was the rape incident, which she hadn't spoken about for years. It couldn't have been easy to share it this evening, yet there was nothing in her face to indicate that she was finding it tough going. It also seems as if the whole episode was not that clear to her.

When we deal with early recollections or when someone is telling a story, what is important is not that the story actually happened, but what the person actually remembers and recalls. For example, a child might say, "There was a fire in my house," something which his sister and mother might dispute. That they disagree with his account is not relevant. This is the child's recollection and shows how he perceives life. With Debra, it is not important whether the rape did or didn't occur. She could have said that she was totally sure that it had, and yet she didn't. I don't see Debra as being in a crisis, but rather in a cycle of recurring emotional turmoil. It is, of course, still possible that she is heading for a crisis.

Another point to be clarified was the decision to close the session when Debra was feeling very frustrated. Debra came here because she needed help, and yet helping her is difficult because she is so good at helping herself. It was important that she leave unresolved. To have brought the session to a more typical closure would have been unnatural. At the moment, Debra is very mixed-up and confused. She is looking for something meaningful in life but has not found it. If we say to someone like this that they should find significance within themselves, it will sound like a cliché. The fact is that to do anything, however exciting in prospect, would still seem boring.

I would guess that one of her early recollections or childhood experiences involved either being sick or staying in bed. I have found that people on the move all the time often have an early recollection of not being able to move or a childhood experience of either themselves or a member of the immediate family being sick. For Debra, support and encouragement is not enough. This is why I sought to create a crisis, even though it was a small and artificial one.

I also noticed several symptoms with Debra during the course of the evening. She had difficulty focusing and her eyes wandered continuously. This is indicative of someone who is not able to make contact. She also seemed very confused and troubled. However, during the course of the evening, I sensed that we did make a certain contribution by offering her some information, even though it probably was not pleasant for her to receive it.

I don't believe it would have been that much easier or more productive to have seen her alone because what troubled her the most was not the setting but the information. She said at one point that she felt hostile, but at the same time, she resented feeling that way. Every authentic thing she asserted came with a double message.

POSSIBLE GAINS OF THE SESSION

This was a very tense, difficult session. Therefore, it isn't easy to predict gains, apart from the general support supplied by the group by their mere presence, which was reassuring. Still there were possible gains from the session, not necessarily for Debra only. The first gain was for her therapist, who began to understand Debra's mixing of truth and fantasy, her use of drama for drama's sake, and the issue of emptiness and boredom that is her basic existential difficulty. It is easy to be carried away by Debra. So the information and the limits set by ending the session on time can be helpful in their therapeutic relationship.

The second gain was Debra's. Accepting her aggression and provocation, not allowing them to impede the session, and suggesting but not imposing the information turned the responsibility for her state of being back to her. With one-time interventions, the intervenor has to do his or her best, but must also recognize unresolved issues and agree to let them stay unresolved.

8

Connie: Coping with a Death Sentence

INTRODUCTION

Connie, a woman in her late 60s, was invited by her oncologist, who participated in the workshop. Knowing her well over a period of a few months, he was now supporting her through the crisis caused by the recurrence of her cancer. As a couple, she and her husband lived an isolated life. Because of their lack of social involvement, which is the way they had been all their lives, there was a great need for us to intervene and to cheer Connie up by listening and sharing. This came to be the main theme of the session.

SESSION DIALOGUE

[Connie has an immediate impact on people. She conveys vitality, no-pretense, common sense. She is dressed simply and is lightly made up. Her husband, in his early

70s, has a short white beard, looks athletic, and is shy, cannot remove his eyes from his wife. They hold hands continually in a manner that suggests they have been holding hands for years, that this is not a new bonding caused by illness and a need for support. They also look like people who worked hard and never expected it to be easy. They are smiling, in control, and evoke an immediate empathy. Their oncologist greets them warmly, and then briefly introduces them, spending most of his time on Connie.]

Oncologist: In my opinion, Connie had always been a hardworking lady with a life reasonably free from complication, until 3 years ago, when she was diagnosed as having cancer of the ovaries. She underwent a major crisis at that time, when, in her own words, she was left for dead by the doctors. While undergoing chemotherapy, she showed great courage and fortitude and continued to work on her market stall at that time. The result of this treatment was very good, and for a period of about 18 months, everything went reasonably well. The problem or crisis that she is currently experiencing is the result of the reemergence of her ovarian cancer. It has caused a collapse within herself that is totally out of character for her.

[Connie, her husband Bill, and the oncologist take their seats.]

Nira: Connie, could you tell us your story?

Connie: I went to the doctor after some friends commented that I wasn't looking very well. He said that I had fluid on the stomach. Then on top of that there was this car accident.

Bill: The second doctor said that she had cancer, and she was sent to a hospital specializing in the treatment of cancer patients. If she had not been sent, she would have died. At this hospital, they said that they would have to operate within a week.

Nira: I would like to return to the car accident, which you briefly touched on. Could you say a little more about what happened? Before you answer, I would like to make an agreement with Bill. Before we started, you said that you wished to be an observer.

Bill: I've changed my mind. [Laughter.]

Nira: As long as we are clear on this point . . .

Connie: The crash was a very great shock. There was a lady with a pram, and I thought I had killed her. They said at the time that it was due to my bad driving, but they have since discovered that it wasn't.

Nira: You mentioned a possible connection between the road accident and the appearance of the cancer. Could you say a little of what happened later? To verify that I haven't misunderstood what you have said, could you state in what way these two events might be connected?

Connie: Shock. Shock can do a lot; it's a terrible thing.

Nira: I am sure that many people have had the experience of being in shock and, equally, that many people have never had the experience. Connie, perhaps you could explain what shock does to a person.

Connie: It screws you up inside.

Nira: For how long? Half an hour?

Connie: For the whole time.

Nira: How long? Months? Years?

Connie: Three weeks.

Nira: What does shock signify to you? Does your mind work well, and can you still solve problems?

Connie: No, you can't work properly.

Nira: Do you have a feeling of desperation? Do you feel anything?

Connie: If you hurt yourself, it doesn't matter.

Nira: So with the car accident you experienced one kind of shock, and then you learned that you had the cancer. What kind of shock did you suffer when you heard the news?

Connie: Although I was upset, I was not really shocked.

Nira: We would expect that receiving such news would be a shock. Learning that you have cancer normally is a shock. And yet Connie tells us that although it was sad it was not shocking. It would seem then that it is not so much what is said that is of the greatest significance, but how it is perceived by the individual and the state that that person is in. Connie, if it wasn't a shock to you, could you describe how it felt?

Connie: It didn't really seem to have any effect on me, I just took it as it came.

Nira: After this you went into treatment. Tell us what happened to you during this time?

Connie: I was determined to pull through.

Nira: Could you describe another crisis or a difficult experience that occurred earlier in your lifetime?

Connie: When my first marriage was dissolved.

Bill: What about your mother? [Bill misunderstood "earlier" to mean childhood, and this changes the direction of the discussion.]

Connie: She was a very bad mother, and I was an only child.

Nira: What was bad about her?

Connie: She never looked after me because she was so wrapped up in her own affairs.

Nira: Do you think that you are like her?

Connie: God forbid, she wasn't a proper mother.

Nira: So, as a consequence, you learned to take care of yourself. I would guess that you also took care of others. You ran a market stall with your husband. Were you good at it? Did you enjoy it?

Connie: We were very good at it, but I didn't enjoy the atmosphere of working in a market.

Nira: When did you give this up?

Bill: When she began to feel ill.

Nira: It would seem that, but for your illness, you probably would still be carrying on. How do you spend your time now that you are no longer working?

Connie: I used to do a lot of cooking, but lately I can't even do that.

Nira: What happened when you were told you were having a relapse?

Connie: The doctor informed me that I had only 10 months to live.

Nira: Did you request this information?

Connie: No, he just told me that there was no cure and it was then that I asked how long I had to live. He didn't want to tell me, but I got it out of him. After I heard this, I didn't want to know about anything else, it was a total shock. Now, I seem to have pulled myself together and try to take things as they come.

Nira: How do you "take things as they come"? What do you do with your life now? Do you experience new thoughts and new ideas? Do you look at things a little differently now?

Connie: No, I try to take it one day at a time.

Nira: What are the good days?

Connie: There aren't any good days; I am just waiting for one thing.

Nira: How do you imagine that one thing?

Bill: She reckons that she knows the date.

Connie: I know that I have to go sometime.

Nira: How do you imagine going?

Connie: To die of a heart attack would be the best thing because you don't suffer. With cancer, you suffer all the time. Who wants to suffer? I don't. Suffering all the time is not living. The mornings are normally so bad that I go on the bottle to help me face the day.

Nira: Does drinking cheer you up?

Connie: Yes, it does.

Nira [to Bill]: Do you join her?

Bill: I have my tea and then my drink.

Nira: It seems to be a good solution, and therefore, why not?
    [Connie's doctor, who sits near Bill, seems restless for quite a few moments, and then intervenes.]

Oncologist: Could I clear up one point of misinformation? As I understand it, you have been told by one of your doctors that you have 10 months to live. The truth is that no one can tell the exact time that you have to live. Cancer grows at different rates in different people. In some it grows very slowly. You asked your doctor for a guess, and he gave you one, and yet I don't feel that such a guess is helpful to anyone in this situation.

Connie: But I feel that the doctor should always know.

Nira: You mentioned how you "got it out of him." I can't imagine how the conversation unfolded. Why was it important to you to know how long? If, as you say, you would choose to die of a heart attack without suffering, why is it so important for you to know how long you have to live?

Connie: Because you want to do certain things, to write a will and leave all the money to your boyfriend. [Laughter.] You do all the good things and give the housework up.

Nira: In essence, you are saying that you need time to sort out your affairs. This is opposing sudden death. So what does it mean to sort out your affairs? And what needs sorting out?

Connie: When you know that you are going to die at a certain time, your life is over. You go out and you see a new outfit, but you say, "What's the point?" because you are never going to wear it.

Nira: What you're saying reminds me of a TV program about a man who had only 6 months to live. The film depicted the moral of what a man can achieve when he has nothing to lose. At the end of the 6 months, the man's attitude toward life and himself was totally different. He was going to do everything. If he wanted to buy something, he would buy it and enjoy it without worrying about saving money; he would take each day as it came. And he survived.

Connie: But you have to have that kind of nature to do those things.

Nira: When you experience a crisis, sometimes your nature changes.

Connie: I don't think that you can ever change a person's nature.

Nira: Are you a thrifty person?

Connie: Yes, we worked very hard and saved every penny because we were usually too tired to spend it.

Nira: Is there anything which you have ever dreamt about doing? Have you ever done any traveling out of England?

Connie: Yes, but it doesn't appeal to me now.

Nira: Did you ever have time to meet friends and create a social life for yourselves?

Connie: Yes, we had a little social life and sometimes had parties.

Nira: Do you still see your friends?

Connie: Yes, more than ever; we have some very good friends.

Nira: Could you share a bit more about this with us? This is an important point, because at a time like this, some friends become closer and some just alienate themselves.

Connie: We have a bungalow in Brighton and our next door neighbor often phones to see how I am. She's a very good friend—she's marvelous.

Nira: Do you have another friend?

Connie: Yes, and he would do anything for me. All I would need to do is pick up the phone, and he would come immediately.

Nira: All right then, you have two good friends.

Connie: Yes, and my sister-in-law and my brother-in-law.

Nira: How is it so many people love you?

Connie: Maybe it's because I have a bit of money stashed away. [Laughter.]

Nira [pointing to Bill]: How about this friend? It would seem that you have gone through this together. Has he changed?

Connie: Yes, he has changed.

Nira: So change is possible. [To Bill:] In what ways have you changed?

Bill: I am very sad to see her in this condition. She has slowed down and I don't like to see it—it's very upsetting.

Nira: Have you reversed roles?

Bill: Not really. She still looks after me and does as much as she can.

Nira: What else has changed between the two of you?

Bill: Nothing much.

Nira: Connie, are you still running everything?

Connie: I do as much as I can, but not as much as I would like to do. I would like to do everything properly.

Bill: We used to walk a lot, but not now.

Nira: Why have you stopped walking now?

Bill: She doesn't want to walk anymore.

Nira: When will you next be going to Brighton?

Bill: We don't know whether she will be fit enough to go.

Nira: How fit do you need to be to travel to Brighton?

Bill: We may go down next week, just for a day.

Nira: Connie, let us go back in time to when you said, "You

need to sort out what you want." Have you been doing any
  sorting out?

Connie: Yes, I have been sorting out my old clothes to give
  them away.

Nira: What else?

Connie: There is nothing really to do other than live one day
  to the next.

   [Silence.]

Nira: Is it possible to have other interests apart from living
  one day to the next?

Connie: I like to go out and spend money.

Nira: On what?

Connie: Nice things, perhaps something to wear.

Nira: Have you seen something that you like?

Connie: No.

Nira: But it would give you pleasure.

Connie: Probably for a little while.

Nira: That's something. Is there anything else?

Connie: We both like jazz.

Nira: Do you listen at home or go to concerts?

Bill: We used to go to concerts.

Connie: If you listen to music, you have to listen to good music.

Nira: Something that gives you pleasure. Do you enjoy reading?

Bill: She has lots of cookery books.

Nira [to Connie]: Do you enjoy cooking?

Connie: Yes.

Nira: What else gives you pleasure?

Connie: Gardening.

Nira: You seem to be a very active person. You take pleasure
  in doing things rather than lying down and being passive.

Connie: The doctors have cheered me up. They have given me
  tablets, and they are marvelous.

Nira: This is an important thing, you know, to get help. Some
  people have a very hard time with this. They don't allow
  others to help them.

Connie: Why is that?

Nira: Some people feel that to be helped is to put themselves
  in an inferior position. Many individuals choose to be help-

ers and yet won't allow themselves to be helped by others. It is a very positive step if you need help and are ready to accept it.

Connie: But there are many doctors who aren't helpful at all.

Nira: How do you feel sitting here and talking to us?

Connie: Very relaxed.

Nira: It actually doesn't take much to relax you because you are very good natured. What we are exploring here is some way of giving meaning to Connie's present life. She doesn't have to agree, and even if she says she doesn't have any time or isn't very enthusiastic, I know that she will go away and think about what we have said. Does the group have any suggestions?

Group: I don't want you to change. You have made us laugh so much today. I envisage people visiting you, and after cooking for them, you then show them your garden. I just hope for more of the same.

Group: Have you ever been on the London Walks? You are taken around by a guide and have the opportunity to meet people and find out some of the history of interesting places in the city. If you would be interested, I can send you a schedule of these walks.

Group: I get the feeling that you have spent most of your life giving and doing things for other people. I am sure that it is hard now to be in a position of having to receive more and being able to give less. Join the club. I, for one, am just as bad. Listening to you, what I would like to connect with is the realization of the importance of allowing others to give. There is something in the receiving that is more special than the giving. Sit back and allow people to give. See how it feels to try something new.

[Connie gets up from her seat and is embraced by Nira and the open arms of the group. Bill is crying.]

POSSIBLE GAINS OF THE SESSION

Nira [to the group]: Tonight was not a therapy session or an insightful evening. Connie was referred by her doctor because of a collapse in her morale. This woman carried on very well, recounting all her inner resources to recover and go on. But the relapse and the doctor's prognosis took the wind out of her sails.

Tonight's workshop was a meeting of diverse people, sharing with them, making them laugh, and laughing with them. Connie and Bill now live in isolation. Our intervention—discussing dying, spending time, friendship, and possibilities of change—was in itself new material and a new situation for them. The laughter was a sign of dialogue between them and the group. It is rather odd and unexpected to intervene in a cancer case after a relapse when depression and anxiety are strong and find ourselves laughing, enjoying, and even being encouraged by a sick person.

9

Richard and Susan: Anxiety in the Face of Terminal Cancer

INTRODUCTION

Richard and Susan, by their very presence and conduct, will remain indelibly alive in the memory of all the participants of this workshop. Richard, though dying and overtaken by anxiety, was at the same time self-analyzing and controlling. They were a team, and now, with the recurrence of cancer, they faced a crisis together and asked for intervention. This session prompted us, more than anything else, to reflect back to them the strength they have in their love and their ability to recharge from it in the face of death and separation.

SESSION DIALOGUE

[The oncologist introduces Richard and Susan. He seems to be very familiar and close to the couple. He sits next to them, talks frankly, with pained expression. The main reason they were invited to come was Richard's uncontrolled anxiety.

Richard is a strongly built man, with an open face, direct look, a person whom you trust immediately. He is holding hands with Susan, as if letting go of her hand will cause him to lose direction. Susan is in her mid-40s, dressed youthful and "sportish." Her face reveals suffering, control, and struggle. They seem inseparable. The group quickly warms to them, and they seem to create a family atmosphere around them. After shaking hands, Nira joins, sitting on Richard's side.]

Oncologist: Both Richard and Susan are currently in a situation of crisis. Richard is 46 and a management consultant. A very large part of his life is concerned with problem solving and conflict resolution. They have two sons, both finishing school at the moment. In February of last year, Richard was going about his life when he started to cough. Not only this, he started to cough up a bit of blood. Although he went to doctors and had X rays and other tests, it wasn't apparent at the time that anything was wrong. The following August, a chest X ray subsequently revealed he had lung cancer. Further testing revealed that the cancer had spread to other organs. Richard had a very difficult time when this was explained to him. He was eventually admitted to the hospital and was treated with chemotherapy, to which he responded well. Within a few months, the lungs had cleared entirely of the disease and the liver had returned to normal.

Richard began to feel very much better but was plagued by anxiety because his doctors couldn't say categorically that the disease would not return. During the past year both he and Susan have had great difficulty dealing with this tremendous uncertainty. In many ways the end of treatment was the most difficult time of all. Shortly after, Richard once again started to cough, and it soon became evident that the lung cancer had recurred. During this past week, when all this happened, Richard resumed chemotherapy treatment.

Nira: What I would like both of you to do, in whatever order you choose, is to tell us the story in a little more detail.

Richard: Initially I went to our local hospital because my doctor believed that I had a stomach ulcer. I also had a series of traumatic experiences. First I was being made redundant at the large company where I worked. Then I got myself a dog, and someone ran over it deliberately. I then thought I would get myself together and start a new career. With this in mind, I went to the university to get a master's degree. Then, I suppose, this happened. It seemed like one blow after another. I needed to have a means of earning a living without relying on somebody else, and so at the university, I chose to study something that was vocational. This meant that I didn't enjoy it as much as I might. My predicament left me with a need to do this; I chose a route to achieving something.

When I finished studying, I came back, did an enormous amount of work, and was under great pressure yet again. In fact, my whole life has been self-inflicted pressure.

Nira: It seems to me that you can put a lot of pressure on yourself and handle it.

Richard: Yes. I suppose I'm really task oriented. I tend to look for problems and to seek their cause-and-effect relationships.

Nira: Before this series of events to which you just referred, did you ever in your life undergo a severe crisis?

Richard: What I failed to say, and this is indicative of my interest in myself, is that my mother also died during this crisis period. Your question about this gets very personal. You would probably have to go back to when I was 7 for anything similar.

Nira: How did you handle it at 7?

Richard: I didn't really. It was painful because I was the unwitting cause of the thing being sorted out.

Susan: I find it very difficult to talk because we have been married for 21 years and Richard has been a workaholic. He was away working while I was with the children. He didn't attend any of the school Christmas plays unless one of the boys had a leading part, when he would make a real effort to attend. He is still a terrific father, but there are two levels to his fatherhood. He has supplied the money for both of them to attend good schools, and despite what he has said, he is very clever and very well thought of at work. So, in the background, we hardly saw him because he would come home very late, we would eat a meal, and then go to bed.

This arrangement actually proved to be quite satisfactory, and our relationship and everything was perfect. Now things have changed slightly—to be told that one has cancer is a very great shock. He rang me on the phone, and when he told me, the saliva just dried in my mouth. It was just unbelievable, and the first thing to do was to get to him at the hospital. From that time, our lives changed because he was then in the house 24 hours a day and began to depend on me. In our marriage, I never got a word in edgeways, and it was all right with me. He had a great deal to say, and it was always interesting. Now he has just fallen apart and is not the man we knew. He is a shadow of a man, who is going around terrified. He has sleeping pills and that is the only time that I have peace. It's not that I want peace, because I would do anything for him, but it is the only time that he has peace. Last week, our insurance came up, and he was debating whether or not he should put all the money he had into this insurance; it's very hard to bear. He is so clinical, so basic and so cold in the way that he talks. I don't know how he can bear to talk to me like that.

Nira: How would you like him to talk to you?

Susan: To tell me he is not going to die. When I looked it up in the medical dictionary, it suddenly dawned on me what oncology actually was. The new hospital that Richard was sent to is just like an extended family, though, and everybody from the top to the bottom is really fantastic. I bless the day that we were sent there. But, we didn't talk about death; I didn't talk about death. I kept saying, "You are not going to die," even though he was very very ill.

Nira: In your mind, Susan, does talking about death mean giving up?

Susan: No it doesn't mean giving up, but when I talk about death now, I am so hard about it because I know that Richard is sitting there with those sad eyes which I have never known. But I know that then he won't suffer anymore. At the moment, he is so desperately lonely and on his own. He talks about the disease all the time, and I don't want to remember him with those sad eyes. And the boys, when they come home, the first thing they say is "How are you Dad?" particularly on Tuesday, when the tumor came back. He doesn't seem to have any feeling. I know that he has cancer, but he is the only Richard Evans in the world. He is so sad and dramatic about the whole thing and when he goes to sleep at night I am so pleased because he is asleep. Then I lie there, for ages it seems, wondering if he is more ill than I think he is. As long as I'm here, he is not going to die. All the doctors are working, and one day, if he hangs on, there may be something that can help him. I think he should just fight because he has great support from us all.

At Christmas my family came down and we had a big party because Richard had just been given the news that he had had a miraculous response to treatment. The doctors didn't say that he was cured, but his response was miraculous. He was the only one at the party sitting quietly and not believing a word of it. We all wanted to rejoice.

Nira: If I try to see the important point in what you have said now, it seems that you have used one magic phrase, "to hang on." To hang on concerns the coming future—whether it be 6 months or whatever. In other words, to you, hanging on is not just surviving but having a different attitude, really believing that a cure is possible. Either Richard will have another miraculous treatment, or the doctors will find something new. In essence what you would like Richard to do is be more positive and look at the short-term future. How do you find this, Richard?

Richard: What she says is sensible. My problem is that I diagnose my illness minute by minute and hour by hour. I tell Susan when my chest is hurting, when my ribs are hurting, and when I have coughed up blood. It really is not easy on her, but at the same time, I seem to have no other interest. It transcends everything else that I come into contact with.

Nira: This is one time when you find it very difficult to answer Susan's expectations because she is concerned that you are continually talking about your illness. You agreed with this, but you presented it in a different way. Let me see if I understand what you are actually doing. It involves more than being busy with the illness because you are used to being in control of things. You spoke of sitting up the whole night and coming to a solution to some problem. Now you are faced with something to which you don't have a solution. In your professional work, you know that if you think hard enough and are creative you will get an insight and some brilliant solution to your problems. However, this sphere is unknown to you, and the struggle is very difficult. It seems to me that you believe that if you only think hard enough, you will find a solution.

Richard: In a way you are right, but I know that even if I think hard enough, I won't find a solution.

Nira: By solution, I don't mean a new medication. There are different levels of solutions.

Richard: I am a hopeful sort of person, but during the course of this illness I have been in different situations. At one point I was getting better in stages. Then I reached a plateau. Now I have taken a step the other way and find myself in a much worse situation. I don't really face up to things, and having been confronted with this situation, I guess I react in an unsatisfactory fashion.

Susan: I have never said that you are a pain in the neck, but it is tragic to see you so preoccupied with the illness 24 hours a day.

Nira: I would like to stress exactly that point. It seems that there is a need, even a positive need, to be preoccupied with the disease. Richard's problem is the disease and the unknown. How else would you really expect him to behave? How can he really think of anything else? He can only if he denies it. If he doesn't deny it, he must deal with it. He is treating this the way he has always treated problem situations. The difference is that this time he doesn't know what the answer is and the stakes are high.

Richard: I'm getting no answer at all.

Nira: But you will get answers. I don't speak now about medication and treatment because in this area the doctors will try to find solutions. People who hold on are people who collaborate with the doctors. I'm not suggesting that you step out of the game and leave it to them to find a solution. If you continue to think about it, you might come to a solution on another level.

Richard: My fear is that I will become resigned, and I don't want this. There is a resignation to the fact that you are ill, and a resignation to the fact that you are terminally ill. I have not as yet come to the latter type of resignation, and I don't intend doing so. I do, however, see it happening to me because I have so many negative vibes all the time. I assume that the cancer will come back again and overpower me because of my weakness. Toward the end of my treatment, I met a guy who had a recurrence and he told me how he had felt when his disease had come back to him. After this—and I know Susan can set the date—I became noticeably more pessimistic in my attitude to the illness and to my situation. Instead of wondering why it should come back, I felt it was certain to because it nearly always does. I know that the more in control one endeavors to be, the more fraught things become.

Nira: Let me ask you, do you want us to help you this evening? If so, in what way do you want to be helped?

Richard: I need to be helped to be better adjusted.

Nira: So, first of all, we are limiting it. We speak now of a better adjustment to the present situation. What would be a better adjustment?

Richard: To be able to be happy.

Nira: Is this realistic? It is very important to be clear on this point because if you are trying to help someone to achieve something that you know to be impossible, then you are not helping at all. Is there any chance for Richard to be happy right now, given the situation in which he finds himself? Before attempting to answer this question, one must first ask Richard what he meant by the word *happy*.

Richard: I suppose that I meant not being so unhappy. First I have to analyze why I am so unhappy and how much pain I am actually in.

Nira: We are not concerned so much with analysis, but with more appropriate courses of action. We have agreed that happiness is perhaps a high expectation for the moment because how is it possible to be happy when you are, at the same time, very worried? So we don't speak about happiness; however—and this is not just playing with words—we speak about being less unhappy. In what other way would you like to be helped?

Richard: I suppose I would like to help Susan cope with things. She copes manfully, but everyday it is the same diet between the pair of us. This is not fair or adequate from her standpoint. I don't think about it enough because most of the time I am thinking about myself. If I weren't so ill, I'd say that I was being very boring.

Nira: In what way would you like Susan to cope with you?

Richard: I suppose that I would like her to be happier.

Nira: How do you think she could be happier?

Richard: I suppose she could be happier if I got back to fighting things more positively.

Nira: I am not sure whether this can realistically happen during the coming week. We are talking about now because the last couple of days have been very stressful for you both. Susan cannot be happy because she too is in shock; she is assessing the same information that you have been given. So let us forget about happy and unhappy and look at what would be best for you. Let us also forget about life being fair because it is not. How can she cope? What do you want her to do?

Richard: What matters to me is she's cheerful, and at the moment that cheerfulness has reached the point of being a bit artificial.

Nira: If I have understood you correctly, you feel it is very difficult for Susan to have a separate life. She lives in the same house, is near you all the time, and her morale depends very much on how you are feeling. So, if we become a little more concrete about this, she should leave you alone more than she does at the present time.

Richard: I get in a state when she does that.

Nira: Some of the things that you say during the course of a day are rhetorical—they don't need an answer. When you complain and Susan says it's going to be all right, you actually don't need this answer. It is as if you are saying it just to hear yourself. If she moved a little away from you and didn't try to cheer you up, would that be better for the time being? What would you like her to do?

Richard: The truth is I don't know.

Nira: What if you have to give an answer because she doesn't know either? We have to start to know how to behave in this situation. What would be best for you—just for 1 week?

Richard: I suppose to keep thinking of interesting things to do together.

Nira: Could you give an example?

Richard: Going to the seaside perhaps.

Nira: How would you like her to respond when you complain, when you talk all the time about yourself and about the disease?

Richard: I would like her to be the mirror image of my more hopeful self. At the moment she has had enough. I would like her to be the better side of my two faces.

Nira: What would this better side be?

Richard: When I looked to the future, she had the view that I was as bloody-minded as an ox and would get better again. Now her reaction to my complaints is very much if I want to feel like that, I can feel like that.

Nira: What do you want her to say?

Richard: I want her to honestly believe what I say in my brighter moments all the time. In reality she is like me, and if I'm cheerful, she's cheerful.

Nira [to the group]: Richard wants something transcendent from Susan, a real belief. He feels that from her belief he can take power—he can recharge from her. Without asking Susan, I'm sure that she'll say much the same thing, which means that she needs some support from him in order to recharge and really help her believe. I do think, for a certain time, you were doing this for each other, that is, giving support and taking power from a mutual belief. I believe and I hope that this will come back very soon.

At the moment, you are both very low and not only are you not recharging each other, in a way, you are actually poisoning each other. Why? Because you mirror each other's despairing side. Susan, you look at him and his hopelessness, and you despair, and then he despairs. It's a vicious circle. The question is, how do you cut the vicious circle? Someone has to start to believe. The essence of belief is that, contrary to regular thinking, where we want evidence and proof, with belief we don't need proof. In the realm of spirituality, of religion and anything that transcends the material world, we don't look for evidence. That is the power of religion—to be able to go on despite everything that is happening in this world. One of you has to start to believe; it could be either of you.

Richard, you tell us the thing that you want from Susan, and because you know and love each other very much, you know that there is no way of pretending. You want the real thing and yet it seems to me, that you have the real thing because you love each other so much. The power of love may sound like a cliché, but in your situation love is like the power of life and belief. Even when Susan was describing the long hours which Richard spent away from the house, it was as if you were still going through your lives together. Togetherness is not measured by the hours that people spend together—it is a combination of souls and their common goal in life. Before you touch on religion and spirit, you have love. This is indeed a great power, and it is possible to recharge from that.

Richard: Susan's friends have tended to remain friends whereas my business and social acquaintances have tended to view the situation I am in as something they don't want to be associated with.

Nira: This, of course, is another discovery. At a time like this you find new friends. You are now in a different role, and your friends respond to you in your previous role. Now you speak openly about your situation and what is worrying you. People whom you meet now, however, see you as you are now and can, in a very short time, become your friends. Did you have this experience? Did you make any new friends in the last couple of years?

Richard: In the hospital it was difficult to make friends. To some extent, the others in the ward are rivals because only so many people can get better. I was friendly with one guy who got better and I know that when he was being wheeled down the ward I thought that there might only be room for one of us.

Nira: This is an example of what I call *disinformation.* We have ideas about life and we project them from one field to another. When you say "There might only be room for one of us," this idea is inappropriate in this context. It seems like you regard all of life as a race with prizes for the first past the post. Many times we don't appreciate that situations like this aren't akin to a race. You are on your own journey and those people that you meet along the way, are on their own journey following their particular path.

So let us go back to how you can be less unhappy. I think that you can be less unhappy by using the new gifts that you have acquired. You are looking for a message, and when people look for messages they find them. They can come in different ways, one of which is creative. Maybe you could consider writing about yourself, about what life is like now, about your sons, about Susan, about how you feel. Writing is a very good outlet. With creative writing you discover things while you write. Doing new things doesn't mean getting away from the disease; indeed don't even try not to think about it. This would be silly. Use all the thinking that you do now about your disease and write, paint, or do anything that is creative. This is one way, not only to be less unhappy, but to find an alternative to your situation. You could also consider reading because reading provides information and part of the reason you feel so anxious is that you don't have enough information about this whole thing. Cancer is only one element in your situation. You are now in anxiety and you are limited because you don't work. This is your situation now—it's not just cancer. Find out, read what other people have done in this situation, and when you read, something will click.

It is all very well for me to tell you that with a better attitude, things will improve. But how will it help? In what way will it be better? No one can give you a solution; you will have to find it out. If you try to be creative in new ways, I am sure that you will discover this solution, the one that is appropriate to your particular situation.

Richard: I hear what you are saying, but I think what I wanted to do was to step up to a higher goal, one that is not too ridiculous.

Nira: What would be higher goal for you?

Susan: I'd like him to get up in the morning and say, "Thank God I'm alive, with our sons downstairs, and the dog barking for its breakfast."

Nira: But this is not a goal for Richard. Don't impose it on him. But if you want to say this every morning, then say it. I would like to stress the importance of looking for new alternatives and, if possible, trying to view your situation in a creative way. Finally, you both love each other very much; this is an enormous power. Try to recharge from it.

[The session ends. Everyone is crying: the group, Richard and Susan, Nira. As people get up to leave, hugs and embraces are exchanged in the group, questions and suggestions offered. Nira and Susan hug strongly and silently. All words have been said.]

POSSIBLE GAINS OF THE SESSION

This session operated on two levels: an overt one consisting of the words, conversation, and the flow of information and a second, hidden level of silent communication. The primary gain probably comes from the direct contact with the group and the shared communication on both levels. There was a sense of enormous acceptance of the couple by the group, and the assurance that in that specific moment of time they were understood, admired, and encouraged.

10

Elizabeth: Avoiding
the Pain of Grief

INTRODUCTION

Elizabeth was invited to the workshop by the oncologist who treated her late husband Kevin. The physician maintained contact with the widow and felt the family was not coping well. His main concern was her relationship with the children and how she was handling them.

Working with Elizabeth introduced the issue of bereavement as a reaction to the crisis of loss. Losing her husband at mid-life made her cling even more tightly than before to her self-designated "tasks," namely, to fulfill all her duties and keep "proper" control of her family. Not allowing pain and grief to be expressed created another rupture in the family. It resulted in her alienation from her children and her children's alienation from each other.

The session dealt mainly with facing reality rather than denying it. This was accomplished by interpreting her children's behavior to her in a different way. We also reinforced the need to share grief and find strength within the family, which contrasted sharply to her stiff upper lip attitudes of "back to life as usual" and "each is on his or her own."

SESSION DIALOGUE

Physician: Elizabeth and her husband met me when he was very ill with advanced cancer. They were a closely knit family and for a long time it was difficult for Kevin's doctors to decide whether he had a curable or incurable cancer. As it turned out, it was incurable and Kevin died 6 months later. Throughout this period, Elizabeth was always at her husband's bedside. Their two children, a daughter of 19 and a son of 17, weren't at the hospital very much during the final weeks. This was due in part to Kevin not wanting them to see him so ill, but also to a kind of denial on their part, not wanting to admit to themselves that their father was so ill.

   After Kevin died Elizabeth felt their family had fallen apart. Kevin had always been at the center, and without him she felt there was nothing. Her daughter at least had the opportunity to discuss her feelings concerning her father's death, but her son didn't want to talk about how he felt, certainly not to Elizabeth. He spent a great deal of time on his own and she was worried that he was not dealing with the bereavement. He's a bright boy, but after his father's death, he dropped out of school. Elizabeth feels the family is not right and has yet to return to a state of equilibrium following the father's death.

   [Elizabeth comes on stage and shakes hands. A tall woman in her 50s, her dress and manner suggest fastidious care and pedantism. She is thin and attentive to her appearance. Nira introduces herself, the audience, and the goals of the workshop. Elizabeth explains that she is a director in management responsible for several hundred people.]

Nira: What could you add to the introduction beyond what we heard from your husband's doctor? Do I understand, Elizabeth, that the reason you came to see us concerns the difficulties you are having in your relationships with your children since Kevin's death?

Elizabeth: While on holiday, Kevin developed a terrible pain and on our return he went to the doctor who subsequently referred him to a specialist. The specialist indicated there was nothing wrong, but if the situation didn't improve he should return in a couple of months. By November he was obviously quite ill, was bad tempered, tired, and not eating properly. That Christmas he went skiing and collapsed on the slopes. On our return he visited the doctor and after another 3 weeks was admitted to the hospital. We were told he had hepatitis, then malaria. It was 12:05 p.m. on February 14 that I found out he had cancer and also learned that he had 6 months to live. Because he slept a lot, the children didn't visit very much. But after February 14th, I knew that they had to. This created a few problems, especially from my daughter, who often wanted to be out with her boyfriend. I insisted that she come even though she spent much of the time sitting outside his room. The problems with the children were already developing because they didn't realize how ill he was.

Nira: They didn't realize how ill their father was despite having been told?

Elizabeth: At this stage and in the absence of a positive diagnosis, they still had not been told. Kevin was transferred and it was during the first week at the new hospital that he chose to tell them himself. We were all together when he told them he had cancer, but he assured them he was not going to die. The children obviously latched on to his statement "I'm not going to die, I'm going to fight it." At the time, I was glad that this was his attitude because it was easier for all of us. For a fit man to suddenly become ill and die within a few weeks—well, it was unacceptable. We felt that if anyone could pull through, it would be Kevin.

I myself knew that it was almost certain he would die. But it's easier to carry on if you think there is hope. The children, however, still believed that it was not that serious. Indeed there was a period when Kevin was much better. He came home for 10 days and began to put on weight. This cheered all of us, and only served to reinforce the children's opinion. When it came to the final 10 days, I was sent for in the middle of the night. I informed the children that I would stay at the hospital until Kevin was out of the crisis. Although they were grown-up teenagers, I still felt there should be an adult in the house for them to talk to. Therefore, my sister came to stay and brought them to the hospital every day.

During the last 10 days, even at this late stage, the children were unwilling to accept it. At this point I told them that there was little chance of him getting better and that he was dying. My daughter's reaction was very strange. Although she was upset at the time, she went home and then out with her boyfriend. She stayed at his house overnight. I didn't know where she was and couldn't contact her. When I finally did, I told her to go home because if anything happened I wanted both children to be together. I also told her I wanted to know where I could find her if her father asked to see her. She actually refused to go home then and said she would go the following morning.

When she visited Kevin the following evening, she said that she needed her boyfriend. To a certain extent I could understand this because Kevin was now physically quite horrifying and she obviously found this too difficult to accept. While she was with her boyfriend it seemed to her as if it were a bad dream and not really happening. Eventually she did come home to stay but I had to give in and allow her boyfriend to stay as well. It put a lot of extra pressure on the other members of the household, but it was the only way I could get her home. At this time, my son was supposed to be studying for his exams but there was no one to encourage or help him. The best time for Kevin to receive visitors was in the afternoon. By evening he was too tired to see anyone but me. Rather than come to the hospital in the afternoon, I felt it was better for Ian to be at school away from the worry. In the evening, when he did come, he normally wanted to leave after 2 hours.

In the last few days before Kevin died, the children visited him every other day, but it was very stressful for them. The last weekend was a bank holiday and the children visited on Sunday. It was intended that they would also visit on Monday, but as it happened, they came on Tuesday, the day he died. By the time they arrived, Kevin had lost control of his limbs and was unable to speak. I discussed the question of death with Kevin, and he told me that if his condition deteriorated he wanted me but not the children to be with him. He also didn't want them to see him after he died. Had he not made this request, I probably would have asked them what they wanted. I left him and spoke to the children, and one of the nurses talked to them and asked them to remember what a super father they had had. When they eventually left, already very upset, I sat with Kevin for 2 or 3 hours before he died.

I will never know if it was right to send the children away, but it was the best thing that could have happened. If the children had been there, I would have had to console them. In fact, those last hours were terribly important to me. Maybe that was purely selfish, but I know that for Kevin and me it was the right thing.

Nira: Elizabeth, you have given us a very detailed account of the past 3 months—dates, hours, treatments, hospitals—with particular concentration on the final 10 days. You were discussing two or three topics at the same time. It seems that for these 3 months, and perhaps for the rest of your life, you were almost totally in command of the situation. This despite the fact that, as you mentioned, many decisions were made in consultation with Kevin. During this time you were also running everything: Kevin, the hospital, your house, and how you would deal with the children. At the same time, you were being extremely overprotective of them, always worrying about who would stay with them, who would drive them, how you could call them.

Listening to you, it is easy to forget how old they are. It seems they are much younger than teenagers. They might not feel this but it is transmitted very clearly through you because you are trying to take care of them nearly every

minute. I don't know whether your purpose was to spare
them or whether you felt you were just doing the right
thing. Except for a couple of statements, I didn't get any
feeling of difference between your daughter and your son.
What came across was a sense of confusion, rejection, and
negligence on the children's part. It almost seemed as if
they didn't care, as if they separated from their father as
soon as they learned how seriously ill he was.

Elizabeth: It wasn't from their father but from the realization
that he was dying.

Nira: However, during those last 10 days it seemed that life
didn't change for them in the same way it changed for you.
Could you tell me if my interpretation is correct? It seems
as if they were going on with their lives either by denial—
"He won't die"—, or by distancing themselves—"He's going
to die and there is nothing that can be done about it, so
there's no point in sitting around every day like Mom does."
However, all this management, sorting out visiting times
and so forth, actually gives the impression that although
the family was undergoing a major crisis, you tried, as
much as possible, to keep to a regimen of "business as
usual." This is especially evident with your children, who
seem to react more to you than to their father. It was as
if, in theory, he was already out of the picture.

It also seems that at this time they were not dealing
openly with guilt because you had to encourage and remind
them to visit. It is of course possible that they went into
shock—the first stage of bereavement—at an early stage.
When we speak of bereavement we can think of it in terms
of bereavement after death *and* before death. Many families and individuals go through this whole process before
the person has died.

So it seems that the children have either denied the
situation or have gone through the whole process and made
peace in their hearts about their father. At the same time,
you were undergoing a totally different process. You were
fighting the realization that he was dying and probably
also your own exhaustion. This fatigue is, in itself, a state
of shock. Many people can survive quite well in such a

state provided they can detach themselves from what is really going on. This is denial as a defense mechanism, and if we were to ask the group, I am sure they would suggest that denial is, perhaps, the avoidance of the impending crisis of an oncoming death.

You have talked about the way you recruited your sister in order to help your children. But who helped you? Did you ask anyone for help?

Elizabeth: After I heard he had cancer, I don't think I slept more than 2 hours a night. After lying awake most of the night, my morning routine consisted of standing under the shower with tears streaming down my face, just to be able to start the day. I always managed to pull myself together. One of Kevin's friends was very helpful. He started by visiting once a week and then he became concerned about me.

Nira: Did you have a friend of your own who wasn't your husband's?

Elizabeth: No. I think I was very much on my own. I talked a great deal to my sisters but they both lived far away. No. My life consisted of getting up, going to work in the morning and then to see Kevin. The only person that I turned to was this friend of Kevin.

Nira: What happened after Kevin's death?

Elizabeth: He died on May 28, 6 days before my son's exams. Ian wanted to take them, and I felt he ought to. During the time between Kevin's death and the funeral, my daughter's boyfriend stayed with us most of the time. However, my son has refused to talk to anyone, choosing instead to spend many hours alone in the garden. This obviously was his escape. Tonight, when he asked me where I was going and why, I felt that this could be an opportunity for him to tell someone how he felt. He refused to come with me, saying he didn't want to talk to anybody. Just as I was about to leave, he said, "Well, I miss Dad a lot more now than when he died." That was the first comment he's made about missing his father since May 28th.

Nira: Since Kevin's death, you have become a family of three. What changes have happened to your family?

Elizabeth: We used to be a very close-knit family. The children had their friends, but we spent many weekends doing things together. When he died, we became three separate individuals following totally separate grief patterns and getting very little comfort from each other. My son wouldn't talk at all and my daughter found her boyfriend more comforting than her mother. This left me feeling totally alone. However, I am quite outgoing, and rather than be miserable, I began to involve myself with other things. When I was asked out socially, I would always ask the children whether they wanted to come. My daughter was always going out with her boyfriend and my son invariably said no.

After turning down the first couple of invitations, I realized that I couldn't continue to do this because he always said no. He said he didn't mind staying in the house on his own. Our house was a problem because Kevin and I spent long hours fixing it up. Now when I spend long periods alone in it, I get very depressed. One particular Sunday, I left my son for a whole day and he seemed quite happy about it.

Nira: You mentioned that your daughter finds comfort with her boyfriend, and your son doesn't talk about it to you at all. Did you at any time seek to find comfort with them? At such a time of stress did you choose them for comfort?

Elizabeth: They found it very difficult to talk to me because they didn't want to upset me.

Nira: In a way then, there is a kind of mutual overprotection. The purpose of this protection is to avoid pain but the cost is distance. You are unable to find comfort in them and they are unable to find it in you. You may, of course, still pretend that you can grieve in your own way, but you dropped an important clue tonight when you spoke to your son. You opened up to him and, in saying that you were going for consultation over your difficulty, you gave him some very intimate information. He responded to this immediately.

Elizabeth: But I've sat with him on many occasions and asked him if there was anything he wanted to talk about. His response is always that he doesn't want to talk about it to anyone. All we do is talk about general things, and now that he has started to opt out, some of our discussions have been quite heated.

Nira: Is there anything that you would like to change about the current situation?

Elizabeth: I would like them to be able to confide in me.

Nira: Let me see if I can clear up your message. When you say that you want them to confide, does that mean that you would accept their behavior, and you only want them to share? Or do you mean that you want them to confide in your guidance of their whereabouts? Or does it mean that you need them and you don't let them feel it, which means that you have difficulty in confiding in them?

Elizabeth: I want my children to do whatever they would have done had we been a complete family. I don't want them to feel that they have to stay because of me.

Nira: What does it mean to be a complete family?

Elizabeth: Well, we are not a complete family, and I can't make it one, can I?

Nira: Of course, Kevin is missing. But it is possible for a family to be complete after someone dies. It's rather like troops regrouping after a battle. They are released from their previous roles and have to move over to take the part of the missing person.

Elizabeth: On the day of the funeral, I was anxious for certain people not to tell my son that now he is the "man of the family" and must now look after his mother and sister. To me he is still the baby of the household and there is no way he could ever replace Kevin. The last thing I want him to do is to take over the role of the missing person.

Nira: Was there a suggestion in my last statement that your son should take Kevin's place? Would you accept that now that he is gone none of you will be the same?

Elizabeth: Yes, none of us are the same.

Nira: Now that none of you can be the same, and that includes your son Ian, he cannot stay the baby he used to be.

Elizabeth: My problem is that I want him to realize that I can cope quite easily. I don't want him to take over all the masculine roles. I can quite well manage all that. Otherwise he will feel tied to me and I don't want that. I want him to feel as free as if he had two parents.

Nira: But he doesn't have two parents. If we can assist you in any way, it will, I feel, be by helping you to look at things from a different angle. There is a very clear double message. On the one hand, the situation is totally different. Kevin isn't there anymore and no one can replace him. However, you also say that you want everything to be as if there were still two parents. You're saying, "I don't want my two children to be overburdened or my son to have to take care of his invalid mother. I want to behave as if everything is all right, and *as if nothing really happened.*" You are also saying that you don't want your son to take on all the traditional masculine responsibilities. Who will take them on? You. You are winning because you are saying these are your roles, not his, and then you take over. You are saying in effect to your son, a young man of 17, that he is a baby and not a man, and that he shouldn't become attached to you. But actually you are detaching from him. Perhaps, now that Kevin is not around, your son is actually growing up a bit faster.

Elizabeth: Yes, he should be.

Nira: Will you let him? Although growing up is a natural process, we still need to be allowed to grow up. It seems that you want Ian to fulfill his duties but not to respond to his father's death. Since you mentioned confiding, it seems that you really doubt his ability to cope well. That goes for your daughter as well. I have the impression that, unlike your son, your daughter has made it clear that she is on her own and that you have little say in what she and her boyfriend decide to do.

Elizabeth: Yes, that is very much the case.

Nira: You had a very strong grip on your son.

Elizabeth: But clearly it was not strong enough if he could just throw in the towel and walk out of school. Although he is growing up fast, his attitude in some matters is obviously very immature. He has failed his exams and walked out of school.

Nira: I realize that we come from different cultures, but basically life is the same everywhere. When I heard you talking about your husband's funeral, there seemed to be a very clear message. Despite the very stressful time for all of you, it was important that your son continue preparing for his exams. Why is it such a bizarre phenomenon that your son, then 16 and just having lost his father, failed in school? His priorities are changing and he is growing up. This is a painful process.

Like all youngsters his age, he is a bit egotistical and he is also depressed. While his priorities are changing, he is getting an unclear message from you. He doesn't know what you want from him. You want him to grow up but only in regard to his succeeding at school. At the same time you are blocking him by saying that he shouldn't take on masculine roles. He doesn't know what is the right thing to do, so he switches off.

For yourself, on the one hand, you are grieving because the loss of Kevin was a big blow to you. However, on the other hand, you are perhaps conveying that things must be all right and that you have to get back to normal life. Which means that bereavement is over or was never permitted to disturb the tasks of life. Bereavement is a natural process, and it does disturb the ongoing flow of life because it is part of life. Now allowing it, in whatever form it may appear, means going on functioning on automatic pilot. Could it be that Ian is struggling against "business as usual" and for his right to grieve? Who among the three of you is showing the most severe signs of bereavement?

Elizabeth: He is.

Nira: It would be interesting to know if everyone here agrees with you. I use the word *showing* advisedly because bereavement is not something that can be quantified. Is he getting support in his bereavement or is he accused? He's not thinking about his future and may continue to drop out for the next few years, but then he'll pick up. He's only 17 and has time to grow and change. You seem to be very concerned that it is a now or never situation. He is picking up on this despairing message and is feeling that if he fails now there will be no future for him. Actually what he really needs is more encouragement. Does he have any friends?

Elizabeth: He does have one close friend.

Nira: So is he changing?

Elizabeth: It was 3 months before he went out socially. He gave up everything he did before.

Nira: Because he was in bereavement. How about Andrea? In what ways does she grieve?

Elizabeth: Initially she was with her boyfriend all the time. It got to the point by September that I thought he was coming around too often and not allowing the relationship to grow at a gentler pace. Also I felt his intrusion in my house was annoying. I knew there was something wrong with the relationship from the beginning. Eventually I suggested that they spend only half of the week together. I simply found it difficult coming home and always finding someone else in my house.

In July, when they said they were going to get engaged, I asked both of them if they had thought through all the implications. I also mentioned that my daughter was going through a great emotional upheaval. Ultimately, I said that if they really wanted it, I couldn't and indeed wouldn't stand in their way. Two weeks later they got engaged even though they knew I wasn't totally happy about it. At Christmas, my daughter stayed with her boyfriend and my son and I went skiing. The week before we went, I sensed that she was regretting her decision. When we returned she was staying with my sister.

Nira: How is your relationship now? Has it improved?

Elizabeth: Yes, but she can be very bad tempered. I remember during one conversation she and Ian said that I had never told either of them that their father was dying. I responded by saying that I did say he was dying but that there was a chance of his being saved.

Nira: Did you feel sincere in this response? And what did you hear them saying?

Elizabeth: That nobody had ever told them that he was dying.

Nira: But what were they actually saying? In effect, they were saying that they had not been invited to share in comforting and supporting. You answered them in an abstract, technical way. They meant one thing and you responded on a different level. It was as if you weren't responding to what they actually meant. It was perhaps an opportunity for you to open up. Your daughter made an opening and your son immediately joined in. What could have happened? It could have ended with all of you crying on each other's shoulder. However, you immediately took command and told them that this wasn't true. Here and there they try to communicate and you block it, and then the moment is lost. Does that make any sense to you?

Elizabeth: Touching on your idea of crying, although I cried every morning while Kevin was still alive, since his death I haven't shed a tear. The children have never actually seen me upset. I keep going because I manage to keep myself under control.

Nira [to the group]: Let's look for a moment at the word *control,* which comes up again and again for so many people. It is strange, I think, that crying is seen as lacking control—as if sharing with those closest to you how lost you are somehow means going to pieces. If we maintain our control, children especially are likely to pick up that nothing of significance has actually happened. By letting go, Elizabeth feels she will go to pieces. What she calls control is actually not control at all. The price for suppressing and pretending is distance. She can't allow even a moment of intimacy. Even when her children give clues, she responds with a logical explanation. And her son's response is to withdraw and retreat further into himself.

[To Elizabeth:] Could you reconsider the role of control, Elizabeth? Because if you can flow without the fear of losing control or going to pieces, there is a chance you can change your attitude toward Ian and Andrea.

Elizabeth: That's very hard.

Nira: Would you consider getting help? By that I mean something along the lines of family therapy in bereavement, a process of between two and five sessions.

Elizabeth: I would, of course, but neither of the children would admit that they might have a problem.

Nira: Tell them you are consulting with a therapist who has asked to see you all together. Stress that *you* are the patient and that they have been asked to attend only to give information and feedback. If you don't threaten them, I don't believe they will refuse to do this. Could you consider it?

Elizabeth: Yes, easily. In fact I have already spoken to them along these lines.

Nira: I think you have made a good beginning by telling them where you were tonight. Can I suggest that you talk to them when you return home, even if this means waking them up? Tell them that you would like to share what happened tonight. I do firmly believe that they will be more helpful than you think. If you choose a different approach, I think you can again be a complete family.

SUMMARY

Throughout the entire interview Elizabeth could not reach any conclusion unless she recounted a whole series of events exactly as they happened. She was unable to make jumps in the chronological table of events. This could perhaps be an attempt to hold onto the memory of her husband. It is difficult to determine from just one meeting how much of this was due to bereavement and how much to her character and lifestyle.

Elizabeth's need to describe and report in detail is characteristic of the first stage of bereavement. At this stage, which is characterized by shock, the bereaved is not yet in touch with the loss and its meaning. He or she will stick to the chronological sequence of events because it is the only one that makes any sense. Death doesn't make sense, especially in the case of someone healthy and fit. You have to cling to what makes sense in order not to shake your own system. So people in bereavement, especially in the first month, seem not to deal with it by being practical and occupied with back-to-life issues. For some this is a short phase; for others it is longer. Elizabeth has stayed there a very long time and hasn't moved on to allow herself or the children to be overtaken by anger or sorrow, sadness, and longing.

This first stage is right for the initial realization of loss. We defend ourselves from devastation by pain. But slowly comes the realization and slowly we allow the pain to be. The fear of pain in ourselves or others makes us rigid and compulsive and doesn't allow any feeling to disturb the efficiency of our performance. The one person in the family who responded naturally was Ian, but not being allowed expression, he shut in his feelings.

The second issue of this session was the change in the family. Elizabeth, like many others who lose a family member, regards the family as a circle of four that has lost one member. So, she reasons, "we have to shrink to three and close to a smaller circle." But when a family member drops out—either by death or otherwise—the family cannot be the same minus one.

Every person in the relational structure of the family is moving. Being a single parent is new; being the only male now is new; being halfway out like Andrea means taking a new turn and new responsibilities. Also, the rearrangement of the relationships takes time. Kevin's presence had an effect on the relationship of the others between themselves, and with his absence even that is different. Part of the process of bereavement is the rearrangement of new roles and relations.

The third issue was control. The need for severe control is also the fear of "going mad." Although the situation has changed, it takes a long time to set new goals in life. So people in bereavement sometimes stick to old goals even if they have lost their meaning.

The future is unknown. The present is a day-to-day struggle. So the past remains the most important even though its goals are irrelevant now.

POSSIBLE GAINS OF THE SESSION

Studying has probably been a family value in the past. Elizabeth does not allow changes for fear of collapse. That is why, although it might seem rigid to us, Kevin's funeral took place 6 days before Ian's exams. It is important to understand her need to go on, not as lack of feelings, but as anxiety over losing control, giving in to pain or collapsing.

The only gain of a one-time intervention is to encourage

the crisis victim to go one step further in the process. Our goal
is to clarify the difficulties in the family as a result of delayed
and repressed grief and to encourage outside help for the family. It is also important that Elizabeth got informational support from the group throughout the session and one clear,
feasible option for change.

11

Ian: The Enemy Within

INTRODUCTION

Ian introduced another sort of crisis situation to the workshop. Although he was in therapy and dealing with personal problems, he suffered from a chronic, permanent stress. This was due to a complex of issues that plagued him—feelings of inadequacy, the possibility of being homosexual and yet not wanting to give up relations with women, and being haunted by fantasies, while at the same time, pushing himself to be productive all the time.

In this kind of situation, sometimes a trigger, even one that others would not regard as a trigger, can cause the collapse of a personal system of survival. The intervention was mainly aimed at helping him feel better about himself and what he did. The objective was to change his perspectives, to help him experience empathy from others, to stop the panic

and deterioration, and ultimately to prevent the crisis rather
than continually dealing with a chronic one.

SESSION DIALOGUE

Therapist: I began working with Ian about 9 months ago, and
since then have begun to get a clearer picture of his situation and what is the basis of the fantasies that cause
him so much anxiety. The immediate situation arose about
2 weeks ago when Ian called and said a crisis had developed
in his life. He asked to meet and explained that his crisis
involves his relationship with his girlfriend. He has am-
bivalent feelings about the relationship. Part of him wants
it to continue, and part of him doesn't. It is all linked to
his fantasies. The situation changed and mushroomed into
a real crisis when the girlfriend became attracted to another man abroad. This set Ian on a course of action that
has made the situation very much worse. I invited Ian
because he is ridden with anxiety, fantasies, and the feeling
that he has fallen into a crisis that he cannot handle.

   [Ian comes in. He is handsome, athletic, and, surpris-
ingly, seems very comfortable. He looks out firmly at the
group, seems ready to cooperate, and his manner suggests
a serious working atmosphere.]

Nira: Would you be willing to share the situation in which
you find yourself, enlarging on what your therapist has
told us?

Ian: Yes. I initially approached a hospital because for some
time I have had a problem with persistent homosexual
fantasies, which involve punishing boys and younger men.
In the past, the problem has always resolved itself through
masturbation. However, my conscience has been bothering
me more and more about these fantasies because, for several years now, I have been involved in a relationship
which a large part of me does not want to break. Because
I felt that I could not hold back this side of my nature, my
conscience told me that I was doing my girlfriend an in-
justice. I tried to tackle the issue with her, but this has

created many problems. I thought that the best I could do for the both of us would be to seek some sort of psychiatric help at the hospital.

The problems, however, are still there, and the crisis to which my therapist refers was brought on when I visited a male prostitute. I wanted to see if the supposedly real situation measured up to the fantasy, and whether I actually desired the real situation to the extent that my fantasies had been suggesting. I still don't know whether I desire the real situation because either I was turned off by the whole thing or I repressed my true feelings.

During the last two sessions with my therapist, we touched on something that could explain this. It seems that I possess a great deal of frustrated anger, and he suggested that the boys in my fantasies were younger versions of myself. This, I think, is what's known as a sado-masochistic impulse on my part, a kind of inverted love which is called hatred. By taking it out on someone else, I am giving vent to my frustration, annoyance, or anger. If you ask me what I want, I would say to grow up, to be self-sufficient. I actually do not feel angry because by temperament I am a very placid individual. Yet anger would appear to be a very related issue. How can I get in touch with my anger and obtain some kind of release?

Nira: I would like to interrupt you at this point. It is obvious that you have undergone a great deal of therapy and amassed much information about yourself. However, since we are meeting only on this one occasion, can I suggest that for the purposes of this evening we concentrate on what has been happening to you in the last couple of weeks and why you now find yourself in a crisis? It would also be helpful if you could mention what happens in other areas of your life.

Ian: After recently finishing art college, I feel I am now redundant. I am very much involved with my painting, but I am currently faced with the decision of whether it is absorbing enough for me. However, my psychological anxieties are weighing me down to such an extent that I have

done nothing in this respect. I have spent most of the past
week asleep in bed and am floored by the question of what
I want to do at the moment. I have none of the external
incentives like steady work or a committed relationship,
which we all rely on for motivation. I have a younger
brother whom I see very seldom, a grandmother with whom
I lived during my teenage years, and a few friends. However, since they are all involved in the same activity as
me, the conversation is inevitably about art.

Nira: Have you ever been in a crisis like this before?

Ian: I think that to some extent I have always been in this
quandary.

Nira: What was it, then, that made you tell your therapist
that you were in a new situation?

Ian: The problem arose because I saw a prostitute, although
we didn't have intercourse, it was just masturbation. I
became very worried about contracting VD, and because
I feel unclean, I am unable to have intercourse with my
girlfriend. I feel that I have done her a great disservice,
but, of course, I have told her about that. I went to the
hospital initially, but because I couldn't obtain advice when
I wanted it, I also told my girlfriend about my homosexual
problems. It was so devastating to her that she doesn't
want anything to do with me sexually. It was enough for
her to know that I approached a man with the intention
of a sexual experience.

Nira: I would like at this point to use the group to gather some
general information about the question of masturbation
and homosexual feelings. Ian has suggested that masturbation is private; it is also in a sense public because everyone goes through masturbation even if it is only in phases.
Some people even continue it through a steady relationship
like marriage. Why does masturbation continue when there
is another satisfactory relationship? There are a number
of ideas on this subject, one of which is that it served as a
fantasy in childhood and continues when people do not
want to part with that fantasy. It could also be an expression of independence. In most cases it only interferes with
life when we believe it is a disturbance. The fact is that

many individuals masturbate throughout their lives without it upsetting their normal sexual relationships.

Sometimes it takes a lifetime to break childhood myths about what is "normal" and what is "abnormal." Masturbation may seem abnormal if you are an adult. You do it, but you think that there is something wrong. It is also regarded as a secret, something that people should not know. From there, the next step is fantasies, including homosexual fantasies. The trouble with these fantasies, which, judging from the research, many people experience, is not what happens, but what is in the person's mind. Once we decide that something is abnormal, dirty, criminal, or forbidden for religious or moral reasons, then real problems can start.

So, Ian, I think that you belong to a very large group. I have worked with many homosexuals, and the problem I frequently see is that they lead temporary lives. I haven't met even one person who can state categorically that "This is the life I envisioned for myself." With men, it is, "I would still like to have a family," or "I would still like to get married." For women, it is even more the case. They want a family and, in particular, children. It may be that they never actually have a family or get married, but the immediate situation is rarely seen as being their real goal in life. Living a temporary life is never easy.

It may surprise you Ian, but I think that in going to the prostitute and having this important experience with a man you actually did yourself a service. If only, perhaps, because you finally were able to see the difference between fantasy and reality. However, if this were the case, then we would expect you to be relieved.

Ian: I do feel a great warmth and affection for many of my male friends. When I visited the prostitute, I don't know to what extent I was repressing my feelings because of the situation.

Nira: You have been using many psychological terms. Somehow I don't experience you as a person who represses very much, or if you do, it remains very near the surface. There is a certain intensity about you which everyone can see. I think you use the term *repression* as a very negative phenomenon. In Becker's* *The Denial of Death,* he states an original view that repression serves as a means of survival, and raises the question How could we get through life if we didn't repress anything? It is further suggested that if we repress part of something, this is not a bad thing. You, Ian, mention repression always in a negative sense. I do not experience it as such.

You said earlier you chose to see a male prostitute rather than trying this experience with a friend. This is, in my view, an important point because—and please correct me if I'm wrong—to fill the need to totally humiliate yourself, you had to go all the way, as if you actually *chose* to humiliate yourself.

But, to continue, I still owe you an answer to why I think you did the right thing for yourself in going to the prostitute. After years of being afraid of a homosexual encounter and holding it in fantasy, you actualized a real choice, which is an act of freedom. It is possible that this was not a good experience in itself, and perhaps a second one will be better. Perhaps the 10th one will be good. I don't think that it is possible to make a judgment based on one such experience. I am sure that if you allowed yourself to have several more experiences, it would look different. Why do I say this? Because I feel that you are fighting your fear and not the reality of the situation.

You have also used the word *punishment* on a number of occasions. By telling your girlfriend about your fantasies, you seemed to be punishing yourself, as if you deserved to be punished. You made the revelation to her, and you were punished. But if I have understood you correctly, it is the whole relationship, and not just this aspect, that is in turmoil. If you continue to see yourself as either a "good" or a "bad" boy, or think only in terms of reward and punishment, you actually prevent yourself from becoming an independent person.

---

*Becker, E. (1973). *The denial of death.* New York: Free Press.

I think that in visiting the prostitute you did the right thing. Since you are involved in a relationship with your girlfriend, it is important that you sorted the matter out. There is no pathology attached to it—you have invented your own pathology. Ian, do you ever find yourself acting violently?

Ian: Only in my own company, in fantasy and sometimes toward myself.

Nira: Would you be willing to undergo an exercise here this evening? What it involves is that you take off your coat and lie on the floor. Several people in the group will hold you down, and it will be your task to free yourself from them using whatever method you choose. Would you be ready to try?

Ian: Yes, I would.

[Ian takes off his jacket and lies down, his back on the floor. Five volunteers come forward and are given instructions to pin him tightly to the floor and prevent him from breaking free of their hold. In less than a minute, in what seems almost an effortless act, Ian kicks everyone off and breaks free, overwhelming the five athletic men who were chosen for the task. The group is very tense, moving from sympathy toward Ian at the impossible task to amazement at what actually happens so swiftly before their eyes. While Ian recovers his breath, Nira talks to the group.]

Nira: What is the purpose of this exercise? It forces you to use power, not as an aggressor but for defense. Nevertheless you are putting all your power into action. Ian's fear of the devil within him, that is, his fantasies of aggression, is a realization of his power and enthusiasm for life. By experiencing force, you become strong, and what is more, you become less afraid of it. Repression is abstract, and so is release, unless we experience physically what they really are. Holding back one's force is like holding back energy or one's breath. This short exercise involves energy, release, force, and all of them legitimately expressed.

[While Nira was talking, Ian started to cry silently. To Ian:] What made you cry?

Ian: The difficulty of breaking free is a metaphor of how my life seems at the moment. It is as if my life's situation is somehow holding me down.

Nira: Could you specify how your life's situation is pinning you down? Your feeling is not unusual. Many of us seem to feel that life is holding us down when we actually have a tremendous power. The consequence is that we wind up not using it.

Ian: I'm not in charge. Apart from my relationship and my obligation to make it work, my main concern is the obligation I have for my supposedly creative work. I feel that this is something that I should let go. It's called creative, but it's actually quite constraining.

Nira: Ian, have you been your own parent? I asked you what it is putting you down, not who is putting you down because you are doing this yourself, within your own mind. By endlessly analyzing and telling yourself what you should do, you verge on becoming obsessed with right and wrong, as if they were the main issues in life. In a way, you have become your own rather severe parent. Does any part of what I said make a connection?

Ian: But I don't know how to lighten the load. I don't know how to come to terms with simply being able to allow life to go on around me. I can't move away from the idea of a battle, of a struggle to find a focus and direction. I know there is a center within me . . .

Nira: Life without a challenge is empty. Yes, there is a center and a core, but this *only* comes alive in touch with someone else. It is a reflection of something outside ourselves. We cannot be our own goal—there is no point in it. The whole idea of self-fulfillment and self-actualization was explored in the literature of the 1960s. In the 1970s, this concept was taken further, with the suggestion that the self is not the center of the universe. You are what you are only in relation to others. You, Ian, are trying to do it by yourself, and looking inward for the answers. Inside ourselves, we have everything, including fears, fantasies, and deviations. To some degree, we all possess these, but they are *not* the most important thing. The most important aspect emerges in relationships, through work, and with other people.

You have been bogged down in psychological "growing-up" exercises for a very long time. As a result, you are not actualizing your freedom. If you want to check whether or not you are a homosexual then really check it. One episode is not enough, and maybe the next time it needn't be with a prostitute. Most of the time, we never find an answer to the question Who am I? Perhaps you should limit yourself to the question of whether you enjoy having sexual relationships with men and whether that is acceptable in your life. I think that it would be good if you are willing to try. Can you make a connection with any points which I have raised?

Ian: It largely amounts to being affirmative with others. I imagined that when I said I felt tethered and constrained that meant that I would have to break free.

Nira: But tonight you did break free.

Ian: From what you've said, this is a sense of rightness in being able to assert oneself over other people. In the past, when I have done this, I have been very bothered about making others upset and appearing to hurt them.

Nira: Did you realize, Ian, that you, in fact, are overambitious? Have you ever confronted this overambition? You want to do everything perfectly; you are very sensitive to others. Why don't you allow them to defend themselves? You are also stubborn and argumentative, but this does not mean you won't do well in life. However, you have to move the focus away from yourself. If you are able to do this, then it will go fine. And remember, neither you nor I, nor anyone else in this world has to answer to the expectations of others.

To sum up, I think that exercise would be very beneficial to you, because you have a lot of intensive energy. If you unlock the energy that is inside you, you will be recharged by it. Does this make any sense? Do you feel, Ian, that something has been clarified for you this evening?

Ian: It seemed very beneficial to me to be in a position where I had to expend some aggression. There are, I think, therapies and workshops that deal with this. Could you enlighten me?

Nira: I am struggling with the question of more therapy for you, even though I myself am a therapist. I have in the past couple of years sent more people away from therapy than to it. You have been in therapy with yourself for a very long time. You are your own parent and your own therapist. I think you have had too much therapy and another therapist would only give you more ideas, which you would take away and make a career of for the next 5 years. I am sure that by working or by taking up sports you will be able to turn the focus of your life away from yourself. I recommend very strongly that you take up daily exercise.

Since you did ask for my advice, I do suggest that you take at least a year off from therapy and do other things. Free yourself physically and don't analyze yourself. Try also to have more homosexual experiences. After spending so long thinking about it, try to find out what it actually is. Don't approach it as a question of good or bad, find out *what* it is.

[The session ends, Ian and Nira shake hands, and the group stands to say goodbye. Some come up to hug Ian, and smiling eyes fall upon him. He leaves the room.]

FEEDBACK

Group: When you told him to "go and have another homosexual experience," this seemed very directive. What were your reasons for this?

Nira: Intervention is different from therapy. Ian's thinking about it for so long prompted my suggestion, "So go and do it." Of course, this does not mean that he has to do it. Still, there is a directive sense implied by the term *intervention.* I tell him what I think he should do, but he can choose to do it or not. The issue that triggered the crisis is also very important. At first I understood that it was his girlfriend meeting someone else, but, in fact, it was going to the prostitute. He has become afraid of this new freedom because it is a new power.

Group: You used the group on more than one occasion to help him overcome his feelings of isolation and to show him in particular, that his fantasies were not "abnormal." Do you have any comments on this technique?

Nira: This person is extremely concerned with control. His thinking is colored by it, and he wants to be clear about the direction he takes and to get it right. He is anxious because he wants to be in control all the time. I got the impression that it is not morality, but madness that is bothering him. He is afraid that if he lets go of the tight rein of control, he will go crazy. This is why I used the words *normal* and *abnormal.* Ian doesn't want to lose control for a minute for fear that he will go crazy. I used the group this evening to lift the tension over the issue of being normal or abnormal.

The issue of violence was also very interesting. During the exercise, when he had ample opportunity, Ian released neither all his power nor his violence. He was, in fact, very gentle. He probably has seen violence in his life, and now he is afraid of touching the "devil" within himself. The reason I suggested sports is that it could provide a safety valve. He is a compulsive thinker—you can see it in his eyes. He thinks literally every minute, preoccupied with his long-term aspirations, posing questions and looking for answers where none exist. The value in sports is that the aspirations are short-term ones and you get immediate satisfaction in addition to the physical release of energy.

I felt that Ian is serious and wants to be helped. He may never have another homosexual encounter. Just having the freedom or permission to do so can make all the difference. However, I wouldn't say that he won't think about it for the rest of his life.

By telling his girlfriend about this part of his life, he was provoking her. In Sartre's* autobiography, *Nausea,* he said that everything was banal. Of course, you can take the most banal experience, relate it to other issues, and make it sound interesting. There is a big difference be-

*Sartre, J.-P. (1949). *Nausea.* Norfolk, CT: New Directions.

tween what actually happened and how you report it. However, the bottom-line question is "Am I going to live my life, or just talk about it?" To have intimate relationships doesn't mean to be obsessed with sharing. Indeed, today some people do things just in order to talk about them. Mistaken, misunderstood, and overused psychology can be blamed for much of this preoccupation in people.

POSSIBLE GAINS OF THE SESSION

Ian's crisis was triggered in part by his need to explain himself, blame himself, and transcend his thinking to become totally aware of himself. But in reality he wound up losing contact with himself. The *explained* self is not the real self, which is what Sartre (1953) meant by "talking" about life or "living" life as a choice to be made.

Tonight's session was a one-time intervention in what has been for Ian a long, ongoing process. We gave him new information about the issue of right and wrong, and gave support and legitimacy to these ideas through the group's presence and participation. We gave him some options to consider regarding homosexuality, sports, and energy release. The most important option may turn out to be the suggestion to take leave of therapy.

12

Conclusion

In this work we presented eight case studies of one-time intervention sessions with people in crisis. Because these cases were brought by physicians and therapists who were part of a training workshop, not all the volunteers were in the midst of a crisis. In some cases the crisis had occurred in the recent past, and in others a crisis seemed imminent. As one reviews the eight cases as a whole, no clear preexisting description or definition of crisis is evident. In some cases, a crisis state was identified by the individual, sometimes by the family, and sometimes by the doctors and therapists who were concerned about them.

While we cannot compare the people or their situations because each case was unique, it is important to recognize the common characteristics of the intervention approach, and the goals that took shape as each session proceeded. Not knowing any of the people prior to the session and not having any substantive information about them either, we had to form the immediate goals of the session and a strategy for implementing them within the session itself. We did this based on a guideline that took into account the following three points: (a) the apparent state of the person, (b) his or her willingness to cooperate, and (c) the person's apparent personality priority.

INITIAL STATE OF THE INDIVIDUAL

Of the eight cases presented, five involved persons in a state of panic. In these cases, intervention mainly assumed the task of providing immediate relief. These included Brian, Debra, Connie, Richard and Susan, and Ian.

In Brian's case we were presented with a man who is a "manager" and used to having everything under control. He was in panic over being suddenly faced with his own uncontrolled temper and a life thrown into chaos by his parents' illnesses. He needed intervention that allowed him more time to assess his situation and overcome his fear of making irreversible decisions that he might regret.

Debra's panic may actually have been encouraged by her therapist's belief that she was deteriorating and succumbing once again to drugs as a consequence of an old but unresolved rape incident. She needed immediate reassurance that this was not the case and that there was no emergency, but rather a need to work it through.

In the cases of Connie and Richard and Susan, there was a crisis situation. They were facing death, loneliness, and the helplessness of certain finality to their relationships. In Ian's case, the urgency was also due to his therapist's needing help to work through the crisis, rather than the usual procedure of therapy. Ian was at risk of a severe self-inflicted punishment in the form of suicide; that is why intervention to reduce the guilt feelings was urgent.

The four others, Joanne, Jean and Harry, and Elizabeth, were all undergoing prolonged difficulties that were getting worse. Intervention in these cases was not of an emergency sort, but rather therapeutic and educative.

WILLINGNESS TO COOPERATE

It is difficult to make a judgmental decision about a person's willingness to cooperate. The fact that persons agree to be counseled in front of a group means that they are ready to risk exposure for the sake of gaining new insights from an expert who is a teacher to their own doctors and therapists. On the other hand, accepting help during a crisis is one of the difficulties of the crisis experience as discussed earlier in the book. That is why we continued, in spite of an obvious lack of cooperation, in Debra's case, to overcome resistance and reach at least one issue of agreement.

All of the counselees were willing to put aside their initial misgivings about being interviewed on stage in front of a group, and cooperated with us and the group as well. All came across clearly when talking about their lives, about their crises, and about their options. It is obvious that the case studies included people who agreed to work and cooperate. But this is the same setting we use in our crisis centers most of the time, and if handled properly, people in need will not pass up the opportunity for help and understanding.

The initial warm-up time that is so crucial in therapy is very brief in crisis intervention. Nonetheless, the people's responsiveness helped us to proceed and move the session toward one or another direction.

PRIORITIES

Although every intervention focuses on information, support, and options, these three elements were given different priorities with each person.

With Brian the main goal of the session was to get him to reach a decision using his good skills which had betrayed him in the last couple of days. He gave us so much information about himself, his family, nursing homes, possible options, and his guilt that there was little room for new information. We concentrated on support and legitimizing his present ordeal. Since Brian is a disciplined person, abiding by rules and authority, reassurance by an authoritative figure was important.

In Joanne's case the priority was to give options, share experiences, lend strength, and help her regain control and accept the situation rather than fight it.

With Jean and Harry the priority was to give new information. Information was shared by experts in the group and support and empathy followed. Although we were dealing mainly with learning to ask for help, this was more in the nature of giving information about the importance of getting help rather than offering help itself.

Debra and Ian, both in therapy, both with strong insights into themselves and a past history of crisis, got support mainly through trying to change their concepts of what was happening to them. When persons seem to be so low in their own eyes, even if they come on strong as Debra did, the main issue is to provide support.

Information was a major issue with Elizabeth, as was offering some immediate options. While she did not get much support from us, she seemed to make it clear that she needed consultation, not support. We followed what we interpreted as her goal in the session.

Connie and Bill as well as Richard and Susan were the people who captivated us through their eagerness to get any help possible. Information sharing with them was not so much revealing new facts but trying to turn the session into an insightful experience. Although some options were specified, the togetherness of the experience in itself, especially in the case of Richard and Susan, became a "peak experience" for them and for the group as well. They held up a time-suspended mirror to us all—a mirror reflecting our fears, our aloneness in spite of love, and our ongoing struggle to find meaning in life and death.

GROUP

Although the group was invited to participate in nearly every session, it was not the case with some. With Debra, there was a need to control the session and not let possible extraneous triggers provoke her. Debra was moving toward drama, and there was a conscious effort to keep the session as explanatory as possible. The idea was to prevent the session from becoming a dramatic encounter since it became clear that Debra was on drugs, and although she collaborated intellectually, she behaved emotionally in an unpredictable fashion.

The presence of a group, whether small and intimate or large as in the case of this workshop setting, is a participating phenomenon in itself. Nonverbal communication, encouragement, empathy, nurturance, reliving memories—as well as crying and laughing—form an ongoing flow between the counselor, the counselee, and the group.

Although in most of the sessions the group took on the role of an audience, it was an active one and contributed to the general atmosphere and pace. When the sessions ended, the group took on a different aspect as various members became directly involved and spent a long time with the counselees. As the leader, I found the support of the group was crucial to our effort to deal with pain, loss, fear, and death in a setting that was primarily educative rather than therapeutic.

One final remark about roles. Each person who came to us in crisis turned out to be, in his or her own way, a great source of encouragement to all of us. Some of their words, repeated verbatim in this book, are landmarks of the crisis experience.

References and
Bibliography

Aguilera, D. C., Messick, J. M., & Farrell, M. A. (1970). *Crisis intervention: Theory and methodology*. St. Louis: C V Mosby.

American heritage dictionary. (1973). New York: American Heritage.

Becker, E. (1973). *The denial of death*. New York: Free Press.

Buber, M. (1963). Guilt and guilt feelings. In M. Freedman (Ed. and Trans.), *Pointing the Way: Collected essays*. New York: Harper & Row.

Capra, F. (1982). *The turning point*. New York: Simon & Schuster.

Dreikurs, R. (1967). *Psychodynamics, psychotherapy, and counseling*. Chicago: Alfred Adler Institute.

Dreikurs, R. (1984). *Multiple psychotherapy*. Chicago: Alfred Adler Institute.

Ferguson, M. (1973). *The brain revolution*. New York: Taplinger.

Ferguson, M. (1980). *The Aquarian conspiracy: Personal and social transformation in the 1980s*. Los Angeles: J. P. Tarcher.

Frankl, V. E. (1963). *Man's search for meaning*. Boston: Beacon Press.

Greenstone, J. L., & Leviton, S. (1981). Crisis management. In R. J. Corsini (Ed.), *Handbook of innovative psychotherapies*. New York: John Wiley & Sons.

Jampolsky, G. G. (1979). *Love is letting go of fear*. Millbrae, CA: Celestial Arts.

Kfir, N. (1972). *Priorities—a different approach to life style and neurosis*. Paper presented at International Congress of Adlerian Seminars and Summer Institutes, Tel Aviv, Israel.

Kfir, N., & Corsini, R. J. (1974). Dispositional sets: A contribution to topology. *Journal of Individual Psychology, 30,* 163–170.

Kfir, N., & Corsini, R. J. (1981). Impasse/priority therapy. In R. J. Corsini (Ed.), *Handbook of innovative psychotherapies.* New York: John Wiley & Sons.

Laing, R. D. (1970). *Sanity, madness, and the family.* Harmondsworth, England: Penguin.

Laing, R. D. (1976). *The politics of the family and other essays.* Harmondsworth, England: Penguin.

Laing, R. D. (1985). *Wisdom, madness, and folly.* New York: McGraw-Hill.

Maslow, A. H. (1964). *Religions, values, and peak-experiences.* Columbus: Ohio State University.

Maslow, A. H. (1971). *The farther reaches of human nature.* New York: Viking.

Sartre, J.-P. (1949). *Nausea.* Norfolk, CT: New Directions.

Sartre, J.-P. (1953). *Existential psychoanalysis* (H. E. Barnes, Trans.). New York: Philosophical Library.

Shaffer, P. (1973). *Equus.* London: Deutsch.

Singh, T. (1986). *A course in miracles.* Los Angeles: Foundation for Life Action.

Terner, J., & Pew, W. L. (1978). *The courage to be imperfect.* New York: Hawthorn Books.

Index